S0-BUA-527

"Chances are you were pretty good at discipline when the kids were younger — maybe you even read a book or two. But now it seems like the rules have all changed, and what worked a few years ago doesn't work anymore."

When it comes to raising teens, what *does* work? Len Kageler supplies the answers in *Teen Shaping*. He explores the vast arena of disciplinary methods used by parents through the ages, including:

- Bribery
- Community service
- Family council
- Loss of privileges
- Lecturing
- Parental strike

You'll learn which methods will never work, which are most effective at specific age levels in a child's life, and which methods will almost always work. Yes, you've got a lot of *work* ahead of you, but *Teen Shaping* is here to help you correct and guide your child in the most loving, effective way possible.

TEEN SHAPING

TEEN SHAPING

Len Kageler

Fleming H. Revell Company
Old Tappan, New Jersey

Scripture quotations, unless otherwise noted, are from the Holy Bible, New International Version. Copyright © 1973, 1978, 1984 International Bible Society. Used by permission of Zondervan Bible Publishers.

Library of Congress Cataloging-in-Publication Data

Kageler, Len.
    Teen shaping: positive approaches for disciplining your teens / Len Kageler.
        p. cm.
    Includes bibliographical references.
    ISBN 0-8007-5359-3
    1. Family—Religious life.   2. Teenagers—United States—Attitudes.
    3. Discipline of children—United States.   4. Adolescence.
    5. Parenting—Religious aspects—Christianity.
    I. Title.
    BV4526.2.K34   1990
    248.8'45—dc20   90-35618
                                                      CIP

All rights reserved. No part of this publication may be reproduced, stored in a retrieval system, or transmitted in any form or by any means—electronic, mechanical, photocopy, recording, or any other—except for brief quotations in printed reviews, without the prior permission of the publisher.

Copyright © 1990 by Leonard M. Kageler
Edited and designed by Dave and Neta Jackson
Published by the Fleming H. Revell Company
Old Tappan, New Jersey 07675
Printed in the United States of America

To MaryAnn, Carolyn, and Hilary,
My wonderful daughters *and* loving friends

CONTENTS

Acknowledgments

Books take a lot of time and effort to put together and I readily acknowledge the efforts of several who helped make this one happen.

Janet, my wife, has made substantial contributions throughout. Her devotion to full-time parenting has resulted in real insight when it comes to positive discipline. If her contributions were written in red ink instead of black, the book would look like a "red letter edition" of the Gospels.

Dr. Douglass Kelley, Assistant Professor of Communication at Seattle Pacific University, has been absolutely crucial to the whole endeavor. His expertise and insight enabled me to get "up and running" on SPSS—the statistical analysis software that turned 32,725 pieces of information from the survey into an understandable form.

My heartfelt thanks also to . . .

• David Klinsing, whose 30mb hard disk had the memory space I needed to run SPSS.
• John, Karla, and Trina Lapinski, who read the manuscript during a very busy month.

• Dr. Elizabeth Simmons-O'Neill of the University of Washington for her additional assistance with SPSS.

• The youth pastors and college professors around the country who gave up class time so their students could fill out my discipline survey.

Finally, my gratitude extends to Jean Lush, author and friend, who politely informed me that this book needed to be written and that I was the one to do it.

Using This Book _____ ◇

As a Small Group or Sunday School Class Resource

Parenting is not an easy task and this book can be used to help parents of teenagers or preteens connect with one another in a supportive way. This material will work in a small group meeting in a home during the week or in a large class of parents in Sunday school.

1. There is no need for a "teacher" or "resident expert" on parenting. However, someone does need to serve as group leader.
2. On the time flow suggested below, the Group Leader either does the Opening or delegates this to various group members.
3. Each participant or couple needs to have a copy of the book and should read the assigned chapter before class.

Suggested Structure and Time Flow

I. Opening (10–15 Minutes)
Each chapter is divided into sections by boldface sub-heads. The leader, or other assigned person, gives a *brief*

summary of each section. Also, if possible, any personal examples or comments about the material could be given.

II. Small Group Discussion (30–40 Minutes)

If the group is larger than twelve people, divide into groups of not more than three to five couples or ten people maximum. Each group should have a leader whose job it is to ask the questions at the end of the chapter.

All members turn to the end of the chapter. Each person or couple answers the first question. Just start and go around the circle to the right or left. If someone has nothing to say or feels uncomfortable sharing, he or she can pass, of course.

Then go on to the second question, etc.

At least one question will ask group members to open their Bibles and react to biblical truth.

III. Supportive Prayer (10 Minutes)

Share needs, concerns, and praises related to your family life.

Make assignments for next week.

Finale

Every cowboy who rode for the Bar 10 ranch stood solemnly around the simple grave of Tom Conners. Gene Adams held his Bible in his gloved left hand after saying a few well-chosen words and nodded as his men made their way quietly back to their horses.

It was a beautiful pasture covered with bluebonnet flowers from one horizon to the other. This was a special place on the Bar 10. Here no longhorn steers grazed as they did across the rest of the vast Texan ranch.

Here it was peaceful and quiet. Only the songs of the birds disturbed the natural splendour.

Tomahawk stepped close to Gene Adams, who was still nursing his wounds. Johnny Puma walked away with his arm around Happy Summers' shoulder, while Larry waited in a buckboard amid the other cowboys.

'Tom was a good kid, Gene.'

'Yep. A good kid like all our boys.' Adams sighed

as he slipped the book inside his deep jacket-pocket.

'How come we brought him back here to bury, Gene?' The old man gripped his hat as he stared at the grave.

Adams rested a hand upon the thin shoulder of his oldest pal and sighed.

'I made him a promise, Tomahawk.'

Tomahawk shook his head as he thought about their ordeal.

'All that killing because of a crazy man. It just don't figure.'

Adams turned and began walking back across the pasture of wild flowers toward their waiting horses with the old-timer at his side.

'It's nice here,' he commented.

Tomahawk paused and looked back at the grave bathed in gentle sunlight filtered by the tall trees.

'Tom chose a good place to rest, Gene.'

'I can't think of a better one to spend eternity.'

'Me neither.'

Adams stepped into his stirrup and mounted the chestnut mare as his old friend climbed on to the buckboard next to the quiet Larry Baker. Turning his tall horse the rancher began leading the riders down towards the heart of the Bar 10.

He had kept his promise to a dying wrangler.

TEEN SHAPING

SECTION I

UNDERSTANDING DISCIPLINE

1

It Really Matters ————◇

"Julie, I told you to get that room picked up before you go out tonight."

"Off my back, Mom! You're always nagging me . . . I told you I'll do it later so just chill out, okay?"

"Listen, young lady," Julie's dad enjoins, "I don't want to hear you talking like that to your mother. You know that tone is not allowed in this house! One more word like that and you're on restriction."

Mother adds: "You should have done it last night instead of talking on the phone. I've told you not to talk more than ten minutes, and you were on the phone at least half an hour. That you didn't clean your room last night is your problem, not mine. I expect you to obey me, and I told you to clean that room, so do it!"

"This is my room and it's none of your business how it looks. All you care about is this stupid house. Don't you care that I have nice friends? Just get off my case!"

"That's it, Julie! Phone restriction . . . four nights," her father concludes.

Julie scoops up her jacket and heads for the front door. "I don't care about your dumb restrictions! I wish you wouldn't treat me like a baby. I'm fourteen and a half now!" (*Slam!*)

Julie's parents stare at the front door, both silently wondering the same thing: *What's gone wrong?*

Perhaps the issue in your home isn't a messy room or teenage telephone time . . . but it's something. It's nearly impossible to live with a teenager or preteen without tensions rising at least occasionally. Chances are you were pretty good at discipline when the kids were younger—maybe you even read a book or two. But now it seems the rules have all changed, and what worked a few years ago doesn't work anymore.

Or maybe it's been a struggle with your son or daughter from day one, and you've never felt you had the right approach to discipline. Now you feel you're losing what little control or influence you had. "Granted, my kid is probably stronger willed than I am, but doesn't he see I have his best interests at heart?"

Maybe your kids are years away from adolescence, yet your friends are telling you horror stories of stress and struggle. Is there anything you can do now to prevent what seems to be certain calamity? Or perhaps your "kids" are in their late teens, and sure enough, they have not turned out quite as perfect as you'd hoped. When you see them doing something that you think is damaging, is there any recourse? Is there any way to correct them?

This is a book of help and, just as important, hope. It is a book of help because there *are* specific things you can do as parents in guiding your teenagers, whether twelve or nineteen. You can succeed; it is possible!

And it is a book of hope because you will see yourself and your young people again and again through the eyes of Christ. Through the insights you gain from Scripture and the presence of Christ in you, you possess the capacity to both change yourself and change how you deal with your less-than-perfect young people.

For Whom It Matters

Most of us aren't interested in discipline in theory; we want to know how to practice it effectively. And it is not hard to see why the issue is important and deserves our attention.

For parents it matters because *we want so much* for our kids to turn out well, growing as Christians who will take their place in the world as productive and well-adjusted adults. Ever heard this at a church potluck?

> Yes, my son is a real jerk. He has no purpose, no sense of direction or responsibility, he can't hold down a job and can't even get along with anyone. Of course I'm proud of him; that's how we raised him.

Of course not!

For teenagers, effective discipline also matters because it's their life and their future. A major component of their success in life will be whether we provided the right kind of loving guidance. Certain kinds of young people urgently need more guidance and structure than others. Also, research is beginning to show just how vital it is for the parent or parents to be present to provide this guidance.

For example, a study of five thousand eighth-graders in Southern California showed that kids who spent five to ten hours a week in self-care were much more likely to become involved in drugs and alcohol.[1] These kids became "at risk" regardless of sex, race, family income, academic performance, and involvement in extracurricular activities. A young person who spent more than eleven hours in self-care (e.g., home alone while parents were at work) was more than twice as likely to get involved in substance abuse.

The issue of discipline is vital to both parent and teenager because neither wants the home to be a constant battle zone. Neither wants to don a flak jacket before getting three steps inside the door. Most family members would prefer home to be a place of warmth and support, not war and stress.

Discipline Is Teaching

I am not thinking of discipline as primarily punishment. We take a huge step toward improving our thinking about discipline when we see it as simply teaching. All discipline is teaching.[2] We teach our children in many ways all the time. Discipline is just one of the ways we teach. If we do it right, our kids will reap the rewards of those lessons for the rest of their lives. Unfortunately, the opposite is also true. If we fail at discipline, it will take years for them to recover, if ever.

Like any other kind of teaching, discipline takes work. It takes conscious effort, planning, and follow-through. But as parents, we sometimes don't feel we have the energy to do it.

Ever had any of these thoughts?

- *I don't see how we can pay all these bills. The car needs fixing and there just isn't money to do it.*
- *If the stress at work would only let up, wow, I'd sure have more time to think about my family and what's good for them.*
- *My mom is going to have to move in with us. She's just not able to care for herself anymore. How will we ever survive this one?*
- *My husband and I are going in different directions. Is our marriage going to make it?*
- *It seems as if my body is falling apart.*

Health, career, family, marriage, finances . . . a crisis in any one of these areas creates enough stress to sap our emotional energy, enough to make us a failure at discipline. Unfortunately, about the time our kids are in the teen years we are likely to be hit with multiple crises. Life is kind of like a warped board—just when we think we have it all figured out, it doesn't fit, and we feel out of control.

If you've felt that way, there's good news. It is possible to take some of the guesswork out of discipline. Techniques and methods cannot come with a money-back guarantee, but you can learn how and why some approaches work and others don't.

One Size Fits All?

Meet the Jones family. It's Sunday morning before church and Bill and Mary are about ready. But for their three kids, it's a different story . . .

> Jill, age eighteen, is still in bed. Mary calls out, "Jill, dear, are you up yet?"
> Jill mumbles from behind her closed bedroom door: "I'm not going today. I'm too tired."
> Bruce, age sixteen, has been very quiet—a model son all morning. He has been ready for fifteen minutes. Last night he was careful to park the car with the newly dented side facing away from the house. He plans not to mention the speeding ticket until after church. "Dear God," he prays silently, "let Pastor Miller's sermon today be on mercy or forgiveness, please!"
> Scott, age twelve, has been roaring around the house all morning mimicking a kick boxer. He's had everyone laughing, even Bruce. His question, "Dad, do you think they need any kick boxers on the mission field?" nearly brought the house down. The laughing stopped, however, when Scott gave a kick in the direction of Hans and Frans, who were innocently staring off into liquid space as good goldfish are supposed to do. Scott's kick connected and sent poor Hans, Frans, and their watery world onto the hardwood floor below.

Bill and Mary Jones are facing several discipline decisions this morning. They know from experience they can't react the same to all three of their kids. And that is exactly the point. With discipline, one size does not fit all.

Kids are different. If you have more than one kid at home, wouldn't you agree? They have different personalities and different characteristics. I have three daughters and, according to my wife, they were different even in the womb! I can't speak from personal experience about that, but I can report that they are different from each other. Our oldest is a sensitive child. She thinks a lot about other people's needs.

She looks after her own needs, too, and is quick to complain when things aren't fair. Our middle girl is one who has definite and distinctive tastes. She either likes things or she doesn't. Her reactions to life are just as strong as her tastes. She can be a saint or a rebel. (Thank goodness, she's usually a saint!) Our youngest is a happy-go-lucky, spontaneous people-pleaser. Others enjoy being with her because she is fun. However, she'd rather have fun than keep her room neat or worry about what she wears.

Research has identified three basic clusters of personality characteristics. Of course, a kid rarely fits exactly into a particular category, but there is enough of this clustering to suggest that your son or daughter can probably be categorized into one of these three styles. Beginning in Chapter 4, we'll see what a huge difference this can make if we're to succeed at discipline. A great deal of academic energy is going into uncovering the nature of these differences.[3]

Parents are different. Research has shown that different parents have different styles of discipline, and those styles produce profoundly different results. Enough studies have been done along these lines to give us a lot to think about as we evaluate our own parenting style. We'll dive into that headfirst in Chapters 3 and 10.

So one size does not fit all when it comes to discipline. But we can say one thing with confidence: *It is absolutely normal for mismatches to be an occasional problem in your family.*

So This Mess Is Normal?

The purpose of adolescence (about age eleven to nineteen) is for the young person to move from dependence to independence. We are not going to brag to our friends about how dependent our nineteen-year-old is, are we? Of course not. As they move out of their teenage years, we want our young people to be on their way to well-adjusted adulthood. This maturation doesn't happen all at once. It's an incremental growth process, in about three stages (see Chapters 5–8).

Since one of the goals of this process is for our son or daughter to begin carving out his or her own personhood separate from us as parents, there are bound to be conflicts. In fact, we should be concerned if our young people are *not* developing their own identities.

For example, some parents panic when a separate identity begins to emerge. We're likely to see it in one of the four areas that are easiest and most normal for kids to express their own identity:

- music
- friends
- clothes
- arrangement of personal space (their room)

I recall some of my own efforts to become myself as a young person. My father was a labor leader—a strong, union-supporting Democrat. It was 1964, and at the age of fourteen I was ready to show the world that Len Kageler was his own man. The presidential election that year was Lyndon B. Johnson, Democrat, versus Barry Goldwater, Republican. I took the bus down to the Republican headquarters and came home with Goldwater literature, buttons, and stickers. I put a Goldwater sticker on my bike and pedaled around the neighborhood. My father was dumbfounded and forbade me to ride my bike. However, I covertly kept passing out Republican literature at school.

That same year, when my parents were showing off the beautiful view of the mountains we had out our front window to some friends, I marched into the room and announced, "I get awfully tired of that view," and stomped out of the room. My parents stood there with jaws dropped open. And that was *exactly* the effect I was after. I was saying to them and to the world, "I am no longer a little boy. I am my own person with my own opinions!"

Some parents overdiscipline in these areas. We may overreact to a style of clothing or music we don't like. We may not like a friend. We may want to rent a bulldozer or backhoe to clean their room. Yet we should proceed with caution: if we forbid them to be different from us in one area, we can be sure they'll find a way to be different from us in another. And chances are, if we eliminate the easy options our kids have, their separate identity from us will come in a more serious area: basic lifestyle, religious faith, or moral values.

These expressions of independence are bound to annoy us often and alarm us occasionally. It takes some wisdom and insight to know when to let it go with a chuckle. (Caution: *never* chuckle in front of your kids or they'll have to find another way to shock you!) We will spend a great deal of time in Chapters 5–8 describing what is normal adolescent behavior. A good portion of the tension we may feel about the need for discipline may simply be eliminated when we understand what is happening in our young people and why.

Never Too Early, or Late, to Improve

There is no perfect family, and there are no perfect parents. All of us share this imperfection. Sometimes my mistakes are so glaring that I have to go to my daughters and ask for their forgiveness in being so wrong. All of us are totally inexperienced at being the age we are. Each new day brings with it new opportunities for joy and success or frustration and failure. The fact that you have read this far indicates you have more than a casual interest in improving when it comes to disciplining your teenager.

Many of the conclusions and recommendations to be found here, especially in Section II, "What Works, What Doesn't," come from original research. I surveyed nearly four hundred college-age young people, who were also Christians, concerning the discipline they received at home from ages eleven to nineteen. All regions of the country were well represented. Findings from the survey, as well as quotations from many participants, are found throughout this book.

The Appendix contains a copy of the survey and all the

statistics. Behavioral research has shown that about 20 percent of adults are "analysts"—people who relate well to numbers, charts, statistics, etc. If you love numbers, the Appendix is for you!

In Chapter 9 you will learn how to reduce the need for discipline in the first place. For instance:

> Mom, I really want to thank you for how you didn't get upset when I told you I lost my socks. I realize I was irresponsible, and I'll try to improve. But thanks for being so nice, and such a great mom.

My own daughter now uses such "positive rewards" on her parents. She is molding our behavior, through affirmation and praise, as we do hers. There are so many things we can do to cut the number of situations that require discipline.

You'll learn to evaluate your own "parenting style" and how to change it if it needs changing. Changing a style that is not effective will have an almost immediate positive impact on the atmosphere in the home. The discipline still needing to be done will be received quite differently as a result.

If you have young people who are in late adolescence, age seventeen to nineteen, do you think it is all over? Is there any hope of influencing their behavior if you've failed up until now? Yes, there is hope! Don't expect to be able to roll back the clock and treat them like young children. There's no light in that tunnel! But consider these remarks from Stacy and Heidi, both age eighteen, as they compare notes on how things are going at home.

> *Stacy:* So I told my mom where she could go when she said I couldn't go on that grad trip. You should have seen the look on her face. I never pay attention now to what my parents say. Speaking of which, you wanted to go on that trip too. Why didn't you?
>
> *Heidi:* My mom told me she felt it wasn't a very good idea.
>
> *Stacy:* And you listened to her? Whatever for?
>
> *Heidi:* I respect her, Stacy, and she's my friend.

You see, if we have a good relationship with our late-teenage sons and daughters, we can still have influence; we still can (gently) guide and teach them. If we have lost that relationship—or never had it in the first place—there are positive things we can do to reacquire it (Chapter 11).

And it is exactly here where we get major help from our major Source when it comes to life in the family.

The Bible and Discipline

Whether it's learning how to reacquire a relationship with our nineteen-year-old or figuring out how to discipline an energetic twelve-year-old who's just knocked his goldfish into the next life, we have more than ample help and guidance in Scripture. Of course we can't look up "goldfish" in our concordance to find an answer, but if we pause to ponder what the Bible *really* says, we're well on our way.

There are many valuable insights from psychology and sociological research when it comes to discipline. After all, all truth is God's truth and the fields of psychology and sociology have provided an immense amount of potentially helpful insight. However, our basis—at least the basis of truth in this book—will be the Bible, and the One from whom we draw our life and strength as Christians.

I am convinced that Scripture does *not* give us a club to hold over the heads of our young people. We cannot use Scripture to demand their obedience. Hang on . . . I've got your attention now, right? But let's take an honest look at what the whole Bible says *and shows* about discipline. If the proper model is not a "chain of command," what is it?

DISCUSSION QUESTIONS

1. How were you at discipline when your children were small? Which books, if any, do you recall reading on child rearing or discipline? How did disciplining your kids go when they were young?

2. Why are you reading this book? Why does the subject of discipline matter to you? What is at stake for you?

3. In what ways or in what areas (friends, music, clothes, etc.) have you seen your son or daughter attempting to establish independence from you in the last year? How have you felt about this process?

4. Open your Bible to Psalm 116. Read verses 3, 7, and 8. Which verse echoes your own feelings as you consider how things are going with your kids right now? Elaborate if you feel you can.

2

The Bible
And Discipline ⎯⎯⎯⎯◇

It's an old joke, but it always makes me smile and teaches an important point about the use of Scripture.

> An eager young Christian sincerely wanted to grow in his faith. Every morning he closed his eyes, opened his Bible, and pointed his finger to the opened page. That would be his word from God that day, and he was committed to following it.

> All went well until the day when his finger landed on the verse, "And Judas went out and hanged himself."

> *Whoops, guess I'll try another one, Lord,* and he opened his Bible again and this time his finger landed on: "Go thou, and do likewise!"

> Getting very disturbed, he quickly shut the Bible and opened it again, pointed his finger, and was horrified to read, "Whatever you do, do it quickly."

A case for just about anything can be made from verses taken out of context and strung together. None of us wants to be guilty of misusing Scripture in this way. Unfortunately, some parents base their whole approach to discipline on using Scripture in this manner.

The Old Testament Is Clear . . . Isn't It?

We cannot read the Old Testament without seeing that for the Israelites, education without tears was no education at all. In Deuteronomy it is advised that the rebellious son should be stoned to death (21:18–21). Fathers flogging their sons was part of normal life (2 Samuel 7:14; 1 Kings 12:11).

In the Book of Proverbs we find the fullest Old Testament "Doctrine of Discipline" as it relates to the family. Here is a quick tour.

- The father who spares the rod hates his child (13:24).
- Lack of this kind of discipline could lead to death (19:18).
- Discipline is administered by the rod (22:15; 23:13, 14).
- The rod imparts wisdom (29:15).
- Discipline promotes a healthy family life (29:17).

In trying to apply these Scriptures through the teenage years, many Christian parents have taken a heavy-handed approach in correcting and disciplining their sons and daughters. It's a closed case, right? Unfortunately, unhappy statistics are beginning to emerge about how much physical abuse has gone on among Christian families. Youth workers and teachers are becoming aware of the telltale signs that may signal an abusive situation in the home.

The Bible does *not* teach that we need to hit our teenagers. It does not teach that we as parents have the right to "lord it over" our young people and force their compliance with our every wish. Parents who use this approach generally see rebellion as the fruit of their disciplining efforts. They not only see rebellion in their young people but they also experience frustration themselves.

But if the Bible says this is the way we're suppose to do it, why doesn't it work? If it doesn't work, the answer should be obvious: perhaps God didn't end His revelation to us with the Book of Proverbs. Maybe He had something more to say on the matter of how a parent is to treat a teenage son or daughter.

I invite you to listen in on a conversation I had recently
that begins to explain what I mean.

Mark: Len, you believe parents really need to be strict with
their teenagers, don't you? I mean, it's the parents' God-
given role to punish, and there are so many Scriptures
that support this. "Spare the rod, spoil the child!" Your
book is going to emphasize this, isn't it?

Len: I'll answer that, but first let me ask you a question that
may seem unrelated. Do you believe that the saved will
go to heaven when they die?

Mark: Of course. What makes you even ask?

Len: Well, where did you get that idea?

Mark: From God's Word, the Bible, of course.

Len: Yes; I'm sure that's so. But in order to understand many
biblical doctrines, we must consult the whole Scripture. In
other words, you don't get the complete story until the
New Testament. Heaven is a great example. There is no
mention of "heaven" as the final reward for the righteous
in the Old Testament—or at least you've got to be very
creative to find it there. So, should we reject the promise
of heaven? Of course not, because we've got the remainder of the picture in the New Testament.

Mark: Are there other examples?

Len: There are many more. Of course the whole doctrine of
salvation is filled out in the New Testament. So is the doctrine of the church. So is the subject of the end times. And,
Mark, *so is the subject of discipline!*

Mark: But why would God give one set of instructions in the
Old Testament and another in the New? Isn't He "the
same yesterday, today, and forever"?

Len: That's a great question, Mark. God *is* the same, but
things are different for us. I don't think most Old Testament people could have carried out God's New Testament methods of discipline with their children. And God
never requires something from His people without em-
powering them with the resources to live it out. But now,
things are different. It's not that humans have evolved in

any way, but we as believers have new resources that were not broadly available in Old Testament times. The difference came with the Holy Spirit. When God sent His Holy Spirit to live constantly in us, He also raised the expectations for our behavior. Think of the many times Jesus said: "You have heard it said of old. . . . But I say unto you. . . ." By those words He introduced new standards and (with the coming of the Holy Spirit) the power to live them out. Think about the specific new resources as they apply to disciplining our children: understanding, wisdom, love, joy, power, self-control, gentleness. Without these, we, too, would need a much more corporal approach to discipline. God knew this and allowed it (even advised it) for Old Testament people. But those methods had many drawbacks. Since the advent of the Holy Spirit, we have new resources making it possible to employ new, more Christlike methods.

The Rest of the Story

The Example of Jesus

As Christians, we want to live "in Christ," to live in more Christlike ways from day to day. So how did Jesus handle situations when those around Him deserved some discipline? Let's look at a few examples in Matthew.

- When Peter contradicted Jesus for saying that Jesus would have to suffer many things and be killed, Jesus rebuked Peter quickly and then turned the situation into a teaching opportunity for all of the disciples (Matthew 16:21ff).
- Jesus was in a bad mood after seeing so much unbelief among the people of His day. Even His disciples had failed—failed to heal a little boy. Yet Jesus took the time to teach them patiently (Matthew 17:14–21).
- The disciples seemed to be quite concerned about who was the "best." Jesus didn't put them down or blow

them away. Instead He called a little child to come and stand in front of them. "You want to be a leader?" He asked in effect. "Then be like a child." (See Matthew 18:1–4.)

• The mother of two of the disciples made an outlandish request of Jesus—that her sons would be given the places of greatest honor in heaven. Jesus' response was not to put her down for being so presumptuous. Instead, He questioned the disciples about their understanding of His mission. The other disciples were miffed by the request, yet Jesus did not publicly humiliate them, either. Instead, He tried to teach all of them about what true power and authority is. (See Matthew 20:20–28.)

In these few chapters of the first Gospel we readily see that Jesus' approach to His disciples was not heavy-handed. Yes, He guided and corrected them, but with a view to teaching them. And this is exactly what discipline is—it is one way we teach our young people.

Key Verses for Christian Parents

Granted, we are not Jesus, and our young people are not the disciples—even if we have twelve of them! But according to Paul there is to be a mutual commitment in the Christian family between parent and young people. The young person is to obey the parent, but the parent is not to provoke the son or daughter. Provoking, according to Ephesians 6:4 and Colossians 3:21, results in anger and discouragement on the part of the young person.

This is a good example of progressive revelation in Scripture. We would have to look very hard in the Old Testament to find much concern about a young person's being discouraged or angered by a parent. But here, in the New Testament, we are able to express Christlikeness toward one another, even toward our children, because of the presence of the Holy Spirit in our lives. There is a distinct concern for the young person. Parents are admonished in Ephesians 6:4

to bring kids up in "the training and instruction of the Lord."
Yet this discipline is to be done with a definite acknowledg-
ment on the part of the parent that discipline, if administered
wrongly, could harm the young person—and in the Christian home that harm is to be avoided. How?

The Family as Christian Support Group

If Christian family members are to behave in a Christian
manner toward one another, then anything in the New
Testament that tells us how to relate to one another applies
in the home.

If Christian parents are to be servants of the Lord, any
correcting that is to be done, whether inside or outside the
home, is to be done in gentleness (2 Timothy 2:25). Paul
acknowledges that our gentle approach gives the other
person the space to come to repentance and "a knowledge of
the truth."

A quick trip through the Sermon on the Mount (Matthew
5—7) humbles us all when we try to apply it with respect to
dealing with our young people. We are to be meek (5:5),
have mercy (5:7), and be peacemakers (5:9). We are to settle
our differences in love, and without anger (5:21–25). There is
to be no revenge seeking, but instead, if we are wronged, it
is appropriate to turn the other cheek (5:38, 39). A judg-
mental or critical spirit is not appropriate either (7:1–5).

Of course (and you knew this was coming, didn't you?),
we are to show the fruit of the Spirit as we parent. Paul did
not compartmentalize the believer's behavior into that which
is appropriate inside the home and other behavior for outside. If we are believers, and the Holy Spirit is functioning
through our lives, then this wonderful fruit (love, joy, peace,
etc.) should be in evidence no matter where we are—even in
the home. Even after a hard day at the office. Even when the
car breaks down. Even when we've got a sore throat. Even
when we've had a bad day.

Impossible? Of course it is, and that is the beauty of the
Christian life, whether at home or away from home. It is

supposed to be impossible, because then the only realistic alternative we have is to step aside and let Christ do what He has wanted to do all along: live through us completely.

The fruit of the Spirit doesn't come as we grit our teeth and try our best. It comes as a result of being in love with Jesus Christ and seeking Him above all else.

Do you need more patience at home? For goodness sakes, don't pray for patience! Pray for a deeper love for Christ and more understanding as to who He is. As you fall more deeply in love with Him, and worship Him more, the issue of patience will eventually become a nonissue. You'll become more Christlike, and being more patient is a natural outflow of your relationship with Him.[1]

Instead of praying that you'll be a better Christian today, pray that the Lord will really enjoy you today. Pray that you'll be the kind of person who will make Him smile. Think of Him as One who not only loves you but *likes you* too. Look forward to time with Him as you would the most enjoyable thing you can think of.

As we think of our Christian life in these terms, we set the stage so guiding and correcting our young people can be done in His kind of love.

But you know, even parenting with the presence and power of the Lord in our lives will have its moments of tension and stress. Discipline, like any kind of teaching, takes work and conscious effort. Occasional frustration is guaranteed. We are human. Our spouse is human. Our kids are all too human. We need to remind ourselves that it is worth the effort to try to be a good parent when it comes to guiding our kids. Loving discipline may cost us something, but our kids will reap the rewards the rest of their lives.

Worth the Hassle

Jim and Karen Barns sat in the family room watching the flames dying in their wood stove. It was a tranquil scene now, but it sure wasn't two hours earlier. Lisa, their thirteen-going on seventeen-year-old daughter, had been very angry about their not allowing her to accept a date with an eighteen-year-old guy she met at the mall with her friends.

"Well, Jim," Karen sighed, "that was rough, wasn't it?"
"You're not kidding. But, praise the Lord, so far so good."
"You can say that again," Karen agreed.

As the scene had unfolded earlier in the evening, neither of them knew if there was going to be a happy ending. Lisa had wanted to go to a football game, then out to a movie with this new guy. Jim had patiently reminded her that just the previous year they had made some agreements about her dating future. Lisa had agreed that there would be no "going out" until she was fourteen and even then the guy would need to be a Christian and it would need to be a group-date situation—not just her and a guy alone.

Jim had acknowledged that it was flattering to Lisa to receive the attention of such a mature guy. He acknowledged that she was very mature physically for her age and that Karen and he believed she would make good choices about who she would eventually go out with. He told her that if she chose to disobey their previous agreement in this matter—even if she tried to keep it secret—they would find out sooner or later.

He also told her, with Karen's nodding approval, it would mean the loss of her phone and the loss of the two weeks at horse camp in the summer that she was so excited about.

"You know we love you, dear, and we only want you to be happy. Believe us, a thirteen-year-old dating an eighteen-year-old is a recipe for someone getting hurt and hurt bad. We're excited about you growing up, and we look forward to the day when you'll make all your own decisions. But for now, please, don't put in jeopardy all that we've got going for us as a close family."

And what was Lisa's response to that sweet speech? She stomped into her room and slammed the door.

But ten minutes later, the door opened again. Lisa came out and threw her arms around her folks.

"I'm sorry for being a jerk tonight. You're right. It was a
stupid idea. I'll forget it."

Jim and Karen Barns did a lot of things right when it came
to managing and disciplining a teenager. Later we'll fully
analyze encounters like this, as well as ones that turn out to
be disasters. A major achievement the Barnses accomplished
is the first of the three things that discipline, properly done,
teaches young people.

1. Discipline Teaches Respect for Authority

Lisa knew her parents were right in holding her accountable for the contract they had negotiated the year before. She
knew her phone, paid for by her parents, was a privilege, not
a right. She knew very well there would be no way, with
what little baby-sitting she did, that she could save enough
to go to two weeks of horsemanship camp on her own. She
knew her parents had the right to decide not to pay for the
camp. In short, she knew she was under authority.

As we guide our teenagers, we continue to help them
realize that they are functioning under authority. They may
not like it at times. Discipline will definitely, even in a nearly
ideal home, be seen by the teenager as a roadblock to a need
for freedom that grows stronger every year.

In late adolescence many young people are willing to
admit, although perhaps grudgingly, that they won't be
"free" when they leave home either. They'll have to submit
to the authority of college professors who have the silly idea
that to get an A one has to write coherent papers and do well
on tests. In the "real world" of work and careers they'll
probably start near the bottom, not near the top. They will
have to adjust to the demands of a boss. The demands won't
always be fair. The boss might not always be pleasant; Mr.
Boss might be going through a midlife crisis . . . Ms. Boss
might have PMS. Yet if they hope to both survive and
advance, they'll have to submit to the authority above them.
Failing that, they'll probably join their middle adolescent
counterparts, working the fast-food restaurants and enjoy-

ing the "benefits" of flexible hours and a free uniform.

Discipline helps our young people respect God's authority, also. This is a key idea in the Book of Proverbs.

"Wait a minute!" I can hear you say. "Didn't you just throw out the Book of Proverbs awhile ago?" No, I most assuredly did not! The Book of Proverbs gives us many reasons discipline is worth the trouble—and these ideas are picked up in the New Testament as well. It is the *method* of discipline from the Book of Proverbs that is absent in the New Testament, not the *principle*.

> My son, do not despise the LORD's discipline and do not resent his rebuke, because the LORD disciplines those he loves, as a father the son he delights in.
>
> Proverbs 3:11, 12

> Moreover, we have all had human fathers who disciplined us and we respected them for it. How much more should we submit to the Father of our spirits and live! Our fathers disciplined us for a little while as they thought best; but God disciplines us for our good, that we may share in his holiness. No discipline seems pleasant at the time, but painful. Later on, however, it produces a harvest of righteousness and peace for those who have been trained by it.
>
> Hebrews 12:9–11

Discipline is worth the effort because it teaches our kids to respect authority.

2. Discipline Teaches Accountability

"Well son, this is the second speeding ticket. You've had your license less than six months."

"Yeah, Dad, I know. I'm really sorry."

"Your insurance rates are going to go up about thirty percent. You'll have to pay the increase from your earnings at the store. Does that sound fair?"

"Sort of. I guess you could have grounded me totally."

"That's right, but I'm glad you're old enough to drive and

be responsible. I know you can resist the temptation to show off and speed. And besides, how will you ever see Mindy if you can't drive?"

"You can say that again! Thanks!"

"But son, one more thing. One more ticket, and your car sits in the garage till you're eighteen. Understand?"

"I hear you. Believe me, I got the message!"

Discipline, lovingly and properly applied, reminds our young people that they are accountable. It's one of life's crucial lessons that one cannot live successfully without.

In real life, when you don't pay the rent or the mortgage, you're on the street. Forget a few car payments, and you've nothing to drive. Forget that bills have to be paid for little conveniences like power, water, sewer, garbage removal, etc., and you'll soon be without.

The lesson that discipline teaches accountability is all over the pages of *both* Old and New Testaments. God tried hard to help the Jews remember to whom they owed their lives in Deuteronomy. They were forever forgetting that God had an opinion about their behavior, and He constantly had to allow bad things to come their way. It taught them they were accountable to Him.

Ananias and Sapphira forgot they were accountable to God in Acts 5. Their untimely death was a timely reminder to the whole church that we are accountable as believers to Him who made us.

As we guide and gently correct our young people, we remind them that they are accountable.

3. Discipline Teaches Control of Impulses

Mrs. Kile stared at her daughter in disbelief. "You did what with your clothes money?"

"I bought this real nice tape player. See, it has cassette and CD, both. It sounds great and it was on sale. I got a few CDs too. Even Christian ones, Mom! I know you don't like me listening to the trash on the radio."

"Well, Kim, I decided to give you your clothing allowance in six-month lump sums so you'd have enough to buy a ski coat and the other stuff you said you needed."

"But this was such a great sale! I shopped carefully. You're not going to make me take it back, are you?"

Mrs. Kile took a deep breath. She knew what she was about to say wouldn't be very popular, but she said it anyway. "Kim, dear, I love you. No, you don't have to take it back. But there's no more money for clothes until the next six-month period. We are just barely making it on my income as it is. So I guess you'll just have to make do with old stuff."

"But Mom, what about socks? I need sweaters; I need lots of stuff."

"I know you do, dear. But you made your choice."

"And what about my dress for the banquet? I've got to have one to go!"

"I sure wish you had thought of that before you made this purchase."

Question: Will Kim think twice about spending her lump-sum clothes money on another piece of the latest consumer gadgetry? You bet she will. Her mother wisely disciplined her using what is called "natural consequences." No need to put her on restriction. No need to chew her out. No need to tell her to take what she bought back to the store. What she'll do without, or the humiliation of taking the prized possession back to the store after already bragging to her friends about her big purchase, will be punishment enough.

Proverbs 19:18 says, "Discipline your son, for in that there is hope; do not be a willing party to his death." There is a strong principle here: lack of discipline leads to destruction. We all can think of a marriage that has been destroyed by one or both partners' lacking financial self-control, or a family that has been destroyed by a husband or wife whose flirtation has resulted in an affair.

Control of impulses is crucial to function in the adult world. We do our teenagers an immense favor by teaching them to control their urges as we carefully guide and correct them. In doing so we teach them that their choices—both good ones and bad ones—have consequences that they will have to live with, for better or worse.

Choices. Consequences. Hard lessons for our young people to learn. Our loving discipline (our loving teaching, really), rooted in an awareness of Scripture, will produce lasting good fruit in the lives of our sons and daughters. But we make choices as parents, too, don't we? And we also face the consequences, for better or worse. One of the most common ways parents ensure failure when it comes to discipline is to have an inappropriate "style" in parenting. What's yours? Read on!

DISCUSSION QUESTIONS

1. Without sharing names, do you know families that are using or have used a heavy-handed approach with their teenagers? What results have you observed?

2. One of the author's main ideas is that it is wrong for parents to look at only the Old Testament in getting their biblical models for parenting teens. He believes that the Bible's teaching on discipline is filled out more completely in the New. Is this a new idea to you? What is your reaction?

3. What was your response when you read this statement: "The fruit of the Spirit doesn't come as we grit our teeth and try our best. It comes as a result of being in love with Jesus Christ and seeking Him above all else."

4. If we are not growing in our love of Jesus Christ, if we are not hungry for Him, it can only mean we are filled with something else. Open your Bible to Psalm 63. In verse 1 David basically says, "I'm hungry for God," and in verses 2–8 he's saying, "This is how it shows." List a few of the ways hunger for God shows according to David in these verses. How are these evident in your life?

5. What practical differences do you foresee in your family if both parents and teenagers grow in their relationship with the Lord?

3

Parenting Styles _____

Let's take the roof off Fairview Community Church and listen in as Pastor Young leads a discussion among parents of teenagers. It's a warm spring evening, this is the group's fifth weekly session, and everyone feels able to be open and honest.

> *Pastor Young:* Here's another situation for you to ponder Your kid is out with some friends down by Crystal Lake—you know, the place with the high bluffs. After considerable discussion, each one jumps off a forty-five-foot cliff into the lake. One is injured with a very bruised arm. You find out about it the next day from one of the other parents. So, what do you do?

> *Mr. James:* I'll tell ya what I'd do! I'd tell my son he was an idiot for doing something so dumb. I'd forbid him to go to Crystal Lake without my permission. I'd probably ground him from doing anything with those kids outside of school for a couple of weeks. If I found out it was his idea, and he egged the others on, I'd do a lot more than that. One thing for sure, I'd make him apologize to the other parents for suggesting such a stupid thing! Right, Mary?

Mrs. James: I agree. It's punishment that boy needs. He's got to learn not to bring shame on us like that.

Pastor Young: Thank you both for being honest. So, is that how the rest of you would react?

Mrs. Nissen: Wow, I have a hard time relating to what you said, Mary and Jim. If it were my son I don't think we'd raise an eyebrow.

Mr. Nissen: That's right. Kids will be kids, and it's all part of growing up. I mean, I did a lot more daring stuff than that when I was his age. Shoot, as long as he's not doing drugs or something, I say let 'em do what they want.

Mr. Taylor: We'd take a different approach from all of you. We'd sit down with Melinda and tell her we are very glad no one was injured seriously. Then we'd ask her to tell us about what happened, assuring her we wouldn't break confidentiality.

Mrs. Taylor: That's right. After hearing her side of things, I know we'd still want to point out how dangerous it was. I guess we'd start by trying to draw out from her what kinds of negative outcomes *she* could see from the situation. Assuming she would eventually agree that she hadn't used very good judgment, I think we'd just affirm our trust in her and tell her we hoped she'd be smarter next time.

Mr. Taylor: But we would make sure she understood our point of view, that it wasn't a very smart thing to do and God was very merciful to all of them that nothing worse happened.

How would you have answered Pastor Young's question? These three sets of parents are using three very distinct and different ways of responding to the same situation. It doesn't take a Ph.D. in sociology to see the difference, but in the last three decades many people have gotten their Ph.D.s studying this very thing.

What has all this academic energy shown? It shows just what we have heard as we eavesdropped on Pastor Young's discussion group: different parents tend to relate to their kids in different ways. These "styles of parenting" tend to produce different kinds of results in kids. And furthermore, our approach makes a huge difference when it comes to discipline.

So, style of parenting is important. What's yours?

Your Style of Parenting

A "style" of parenting is the way you generally respond and relate to your sons and daughters. Of course, most of us parents do not always respond in exactly the same way.

Picture this: Your sixteen-year-old son has crunched the front fender of the car. You come home from a bad day at work; you're irritable and exhausted. Upon discovering this fender you . . .

Same scenario. This time, though, it has been an incredibly good day at work. Your performance appraisal review went well; the boss smilingly informed you that, as a result of your good work, you'll get a 30 percent raise immediately and another 20 percent the first of the year. Your vacation time has been doubled from three weeks to six. (Sure, it's fantasy, but enjoy it!) You come home, and upon discovering the fender you . . .

Most of us would respond somewhat differently in the second scenario. But each of us has patterns of behavior that are *generally true* when it comes to how we parent. We usually respond in one way or another unless unusual circumstances nudge us to make a variation.

Take a few minutes to fill out the questionnaire that begins on the following page. Don't spend a long time on any question; rather, put down your first response, and go on to the next question.

STYLE OF PARENTING QUESTIONNAIRE

Part I: *When a situation arises that requires discipline of my son or daughter, I . . .*

1. ❑ never ❑ occasionally ❑ usually raise my voice.

2. ❑ never ❑ occasionally ❑ usually announce a punishment without allowing discussion.

3. ❑ never ❑ occasionally ❑ usually expect 100 percent compliance with my wishes.

4. ❑ never ❑ occasionally ❑ usually ignore the explanation or excuses my kid offers.

5. ❑ never ❑ occasionally ❑ usually believe that my opinion is right most of the time.

6. ❑ never ❑ occasionally ❑ usually explain fully the reason discipline is appropriate.

7. ❑ never ❑ occasionally ❑ usually ask questions to clarify the situation.

8. ❑ never ❑ occasionally ❑ usually let my kid have a say in the discipline.

9. ❑ never ❑ occasionally ❑ usually seriously consider their input and opinion on the matter.

10. ❑ never ❑ occasionally ❑ usually change my mind or reduce the discipline I had decided upon based on input from my teen.

11. ❑ never ❑ occasionally ❑ usually avoid saying anything about it.

(Continue on next page)

12. ❑ never ❑ occasionally ❑ usually have no opinion on the given behavior of my kid.

13. ❑ never ❑ occasionally ❑ usually ignore the situation.

14. ❑ never ❑ occasionally ❑ usually feel that it is not my place to discipline at this age.

15. ❑ never ❑ occasionally ❑ usually have very few expectations about the behavior of my kids.

Part II: *In the normal flow of life, I . . .*

1. ❑ never ❑ occasionally ❑ usually hug or touch my kids.

2. ❑ never ❑ occasionally ❑ usually make myself available to listen to my kids' problems.

3. ❑ never ❑ occasionally ❑ usually express appreciation to him or her.

4. ❑ never ❑ occasionally ❑ usually affirm my kids when they do something well.

5. ❑ never ❑ occasionally ❑ usually spend quality time with my kids every week, when we really interact.

Scoring, Part I

Questions 1–5:   Number of "usually" responses: ___
Questions 6–10:   Number of "usually" responses: ___
Questions 11–15:   Number of "usually" responses: ___

In sections 1–5, 6–10, and 11–15, indicating "usually" three or more times would suggest this is your normal parenting style.

- The *authoritarian* or *autocratic* style is indicated by a high "usually" score on questions 1–5.
- *Equalitarian* or *democratic* style is the preference shown by a high "usually" score in questions 6–10.
- A *permissive* or *ignoring* style is indicated by a high "usually" score in questions 11–15.

Scoring, Part II
This brief section has to do with the level of "nurturance" you provide your young person.

Score 3 for every "usually" marked. ___
Score 1 for every "occasionally" marked. ___

Obviously, the higher your score, the more nurturing you are.

0–5:   Urgent need for improvement.
6–10:   Okay, but lots of room for improvement.
11–15: Excellent.

Much more on this later.
Now that you have identified your general parenting style, what does it really mean, and what effect does it have when it comes to discipline?

Autocratic/Authoritarian

Defined
The *autocratic* style is one in which adolescents are not allowed to express opinions or make decisions about any aspect of their own lives. An *authoritarian* style is somewhat different in that, while parents always make the final decision according to their own judgment, young people can contribute opinions.[1]

Illustrated
In the discussion Pastor Young led at Fairview Community Church (at the beginning of the chapter), it was Mr. and Mrs. James who definitely demonstrated the autocratic or

authoritarian styles. If we were to go back to their home and watch for a while it would not take long to see how thoroughly entrenched this approach is.

For instance, if we could observe, we might see situations like this:

Mr. and Mrs. James arrive home about 9:30 P.M. from a meeting at the church. Rob, their fourteen-year-old son, is in his room with the door closed. He hears his parents come home but remains in his room, and neither Mary nor Jim knock on the door to say hello as they pass his room. Melissa, age sixteen, is talking on the phone in the kitchen. Mr. James comes to the end of the hall and stands in front of the bathroom. The light is on. He can see that the shower stall has not been wiped dry and there is a wet towel lying in a heap on the floor.

"Melissa, get over here this instant!" Mr. James yells.

"I'm on the phone, Dad, just a minute."

"Get off the phone and come here right now!"

"Gotta go," Melissa whispers. "I think I'm in trouble again. 'Bye."

Mr. James stands face-to-face with Melissa in front of the bathroom door.

"If I've told you once, I've told you a thousand times, you are not to (a) leave the light on, (b) leave a wet towel on the floor, and (c) forget to wipe down the shower." Mr. James raises his voice and asks, "Won't you ever learn?"

"But, Dad, I was just—"

"I don't want to hear your excuses. You are just not listening to your parents. You take for granted all we provide for you—"

"The phone rang, Dad, and—"

"Don't interrupt me! There is no excuse for this kind of behavior. Clean up this bathroom now!"

We'll take leave of this unhappy night at the James residence. It is a scene that is repeated several times a week. The issues are familiar—picking up around the house, chores, time on the phone, choice of clothing, choice of music, choice of friends.

The Results

Apparently Jim and Mary James don't know it, but they are just about guaranteeing that the atmosphere in their home will get worse, not better. Their heavy-handed style is well on its way to producing rebellious, aloof teenagers who have no respect for their parents or what they believe. They are modeling aggression that Melissa and Rob will quite likely use on their own children when they are parents.[2] They are also in the process of producing young people who will become very skilled at lying or telling half-truths as they try to covertly carry on a life *they* feel is normal and appropriate for their age, but which their parents reject. Consequently, Melissa and Rob are sitting ducks for negative peer pressure, including drug and alcohol abuse.[3] They get little support at home, so why not get it from peers?

Why It Is Used

If this is not your own parenting style, you might wonder how or why parents would feel that they should deal with their teenage children in this way. There are four causes that sometimes enter in.

1. Power. Some parents feel powerless in most areas of their lives. They have no status or authority at work. They feel powerless to influence government or the economy. They may not have any leadership at church. So, when their authority or control at home seems challenged, it feels like the last straw. In their children's younger years the exercise of coercive power in the home probably worked okay. But during the teenage years, coercive power makes family life like a mine field. The powerless have little idea as to when another explosion will occur.

2. Fear. Some parents, in addition to feeling powerless to control their home environment, fear for their kids as they grow up. They feel the only way to protect them from all the bad things that could happen to them is to be strict and heavy-handed.

3. *Modeling*. Research shows that parents tend to treat their own young people as they were treated at the same age. Some parents have themselves come from dysfunctional families where the parents were strict, unyielding, and very authoritarian.

4. *Scripture*. As we saw in Chapter 2, if we derive our plan for discipline exclusively from the Old Testament, especially the Book of Proverbs, we have stopped well short of the whole biblical teaching on the subject. Some parents use the heavy-handed approach sincerely believing they are following God's instruction.

Do all young people who come from authoritarian or autocratic homes turn out bad? Does that approach always produce rebellion? No. God's grace is capable of saving the self-esteem of even the young person who is tyrannized at home. Also, if the parents, or at least one parent, is high in nurturance, the home won't be without tension, but the young person has a decent chance at going through adolescence without serious and permanent rebellion.

Permissive/Ignoring

One might be tempted to think that if heavy-handedness and the use of coercive power is not the most productive parenting style, then the opposite approach would be best. Wrong. The other end of the spectrum also produces serious problems.

Defined

A *permissive* style of parenting is one in which the adolescent assumes a more active and influential position in formulating decisions, considering but not always abiding by parental opinions. At the end of this scale is the *ignoring* style, in which the parents take no role and show no interest in directing the adolescent's behavior.

Illustrated

If we head over to the home of the Nissens, it will seem as if we have moved to a different planet. As the teenagers and the Nissens interact, we'll notice a complete absence of the stress we felt in the James home. We might not be able to pick up any signs of trouble until we watch for a few days, not only at home, but also as the kids interact with their peers at school.

> Mr. Nissen is reading the paper and watching football on a sunny Saturday afternoon. Bob has been at the hairstylist and had his hair dyed and styled according to the fashion trend of the latest rock star. His new earrings jingle as he walks past his mother.
> "Hi, Bob."
> Bob smiles faintly as he continues walking past his mother.
> "What's the score, Dad?"
> "We're ahead 24–14. Have a seat if you like."
> "Nah, I got things to do," Bob mumbles as he heads to his room.
> A few hours later we observe Bob's older sister. Tina is fifteen and she is at her boyfriend's home while his parents are out for the evening. Her boyfriend doesn't know it yet, but a week ago Tina decided that after tonight the "stigma" of being a virgin would no longer be hers.

The Nissens, as we can readily deduce, have the style of ignoring. They feel their role in directing the lives of their kids ended in their early teens, and now the kids are on their own.

The Results

Research shows that the permissive/ignoring style tends to produce young people who have low self-esteem, feel alienated, and are highly likely to have trouble with alcohol or drugs. They are also prone to "standard-breaking behavior."[4] That is, they are crying out for attention and go to extremes to get it. The Nissens' kids are crying out to be

noticed by their mom and dad. Bob's new hairstyle drew not
one comment from his parents, but he is sure to get the
comments and stares from his peers and his teachers at
school. Tina has spent the week anticipating giving her body
away to her boyfriend with the hope that he won't drop her.
She intends to take no precautions. If she gets pregnant, "My
parents can't help but notice that."

The problem in the overly permissive or ignoring home is
not too much discipline but not enough. Young people want
to feel loved and cared for. Especially in early adolescence,
they are searching for behavioral boundaries. You don't
believe it? Ask a kid what he or she thinks about a teacher at
school who doesn't have control of the class. Sure, it's fun the
first few days, but most will feel frustrated, knowing that
their time is being wasted.

As with autocratic/authoritarian styles, nurturance can
mitigate potential negatives somewhat. While it is impossible to be nurturing and ignoring at the same time, it is very
possible to be nurturing and permissive simultaneously. In
the permissive but loving home, while the teenager may
occasionally long for better boundaries, at least he or she still
feels loved and secure in other ways.

Why It Is Used

1. *It's easy.* One thing about permissive parenting, it's a lot
less stressful than the other styles. It's easy. It requires no
effort. This could be simple negligence or laziness on the part
of the parent. Sometimes, however, it is the style that results
from a divorce. The spouse who has the kids is so consumed
by divorce recovery and all that implies that there is just no
mental energy left for trying to manage the behavior of
teenagers.

2. *Modeling.* As with the first style, what a parent experienced as a young person will probably be repeated.

3. *Strong-willed kids.* Some parents struggle with their own
inadequate self-esteem. They may also lack verbal skills of
assertiveness or negotiation. Some kids, it seems, are born

assertive and verbal and can outtalk, outthink, and outblink their mild-mannered parents. In this scenario the parents simply abdicate this aspect of their role.

Democratic/Equalitarian

Defined

In the *democratic* style, adolescents contribute freely to the discussion of issues relevant to their behavior and make some of their own decisions, but final decisions are often formulated by the parents and are always subject to their approval. The *equalitarian* style is one in which parents and teens play essentially similar roles and participate equally in making decisions.

Illustrated

Here we must go back to the home of the Taylors. We may have wondered if they really would have treated Melinda that way after hearing about the cliff jumping. If we followed them home after their meeting with Pastor Young, we would have seen a situation very similar to and yet very different from what happened at the James house that night.

Mr. Taylor can hear Melinda on the phone in the kitchen as he stands in front of the bathroom door. The light is on, the shower walls are wet, and a wet towel is on the floor.

Mr. Taylor pours a cup of coffee in the kitchen while he waits for his daughter to get off the phone.

" ... thanks, 'bye."

"Melinda, can you guess why I'm a little frustrated?"

(*Gasp.*) "Oh no, the bathroom! I'm sorry, Dad. I was just getting out of the shower when the phone rang. I got here on the sixth ring, and I'm glad I did 'cause it was Mary and I'd been trying to get hold of her all evening. I'll go take care of it now."

"That's great. I'll follow."

Mr. Taylor rests against the door of the bathroom while Melinda wipes the shower walls.

"Hey, I know phones ring and you gotta answer. I guess it just seems a little strange that this has happened three times in as many weeks; know what I mean?"

Melinda looks chagrined. "Hmm, sounds fishy to me too. I know, let me tell it to you: (1) electricity is expensive, (2) mold grows on the shower if you don't dry it and mold isn't much fun to clean, and (3) you have a personal distaste for wet towels on bathroom floors."

"Well said, Daughter. If this happens again in the next few weeks, what shall we do with you?"

"How about the guillotine?" Melinda laughs. "We've been studying the French Revolution in history. It's quick and painless."

"Close, but a bit too severe. How about adding 'bathroom cleaning' to your regular chores for four weeks. Sound fair?"

"Four weeks! Yikes Dad, isn't that a little steep?"

"What sounds more reasonable to you?"

"Two weeks."

"Deal."

A lot of things have taken place here that show us what the Taylor family has going for it. There is openness, humor, good communication, and respect. Melinda knows she made a mistake, but her father acknowledged the circumstances. The consequences of another failure by Melinda were negotiated and agreed upon.

The Results

Our style of parenting communicates the respect we have for our young person—or lack of it. This feeling of being respected triggers personal growth and maturation.[5] Another reason this style facilitates maturity is that rules and discipline are explained in a rational manner. Why breaking a rule is undesirable is spelled out, and how violation hurts the young person is explained whenever possible.[6]

Major studies have shown that the democratic or equalitarian style of parenting also produces self-esteem, social competence, achievement motivation, internalization of good moral values, and concern for people. It produces kids who are far less likely to feel alienated, aggressive, or have a need to become involved in substance abuse.[7]

Why It Is Used

1. *It's work, but it works.* It's hard to argue with success. We don't have to look around the neighborhood or the church very long to find families whose kids seem to be turning out great. We know no family is perfect, but we can see that these styles create mutual respect and good feelings within the family.

2. *It's biblical.* Remember in the New Testament we see the family as a Christian support group. Yes, there are rules. Yes, the parents are still the parents. However, the Christian virtues of kindness and humility are present often enough to make all family members, both young and old, feel that what they have is worth preserving.

These styles, combined with high nurturance, make for a family life that becomes the envy of most others.

✧ ✧ ✧ ✧

Is your parenting style producing trials or smiles? If it is not producing smiles, probably some change is in order. In Chapter 10 we will see how it is possible to change styles if we need to.

But within each style there are numerous *methods* of discipline. Some produce positive results, some negative. The next chapter will outline eighteen methods with discussion of how well they achieve three important goals.

DISCUSSION QUESTIONS

1. Share your number of "usually" responses to questions 1–5, 6–10, and 11–15 on the questionnaire. What seems to be your parenting style?

2. Share your score in the nurturance section of the questionnaire.

3. What style did your parents use on you in the years eleven to thirteen, fourteen to sixteen, and seventeen to nineteen? What kinds of feelings about your parents did these styles produce?

4. Some parents hang on to an autocratic or authoritarian style well beyond the ages of eleven to thirteen. The author suggests the reasons for this involve issues of power, fear, modeling, and view of Scripture. Do you agree with his assessment? Why or why not?

5. Open your Bible to Galatians 5:22, 23. Which of the fruits of the Spirit do you find easiest to demonstrate to your son or daughter? Which of them do you find most difficult to demonstrate?

4

Eighteen Different
Discipline Methods _____ ✧

Mr. Scott stopped by the hall closet and picked up his hunting rifle as he headed for his son's room. Not pausing to knock, he kicked open the door with his heavy boot, raised the rifle at his son, and screamed: "I'll give you five seconds to start cleaning the garage. Five . . . four . . . three . . ."

"Don't shoot, Dad, I'm on my way!"

How would you evaluate this fictional discipline story? It worked, didn't it? It got instant obedience—no question about that. If compliance is our only goal, this one is a winner, and every parent should have a hunting rifle handy, right?

Hopefully, you answered in the negative! While using a rifle would produce obedience, it would not teach much else other than terror in the home. Remember, discipline is one way we teach as parents.

As I mentioned earlier, in preparation for this book I surveyed nearly four hundred college-age, Christian young people concerning the discipline they received at home from ages eleven to nineteen. In the Appendix, you will find a sample of the questionnaire, which listed eighteen disciplinary methods. The respondents were asked to recall which methods were used with them, at what ages, and to what effect.

Ideally, the disciplinary methods we use should accomplish three things in the life of our young person.

- *Build self-esteem.* The young person who feels good about himself or herself will not be a sitting duck when it comes to negative peer pressure. Many of the eighteen discipline methods do serve the purpose of building the self-image of a young person. Many of them do not. We will see some unhappy statistics that show us how the widespread use of some methods that seem "successful" actually tears down self-esteem instead of building it.

- *Build responsibility.* In Chapter 2 we learned that the reasons for discipline found in the Bible include (a) teaching respect for authority, (b) teaching accountability, and (c) teaching control of impulses. "Building responsibility" is a good summary of what those three tend to accomplish. There are discipline methods available to us that will help our young people become more responsible.

- *Build our family as a Christian support group.* If we are Christian parents and our young people are likewise Christians, we will want to experience the fellowship and mutual support that is possible among Christians. Building the family support structure is possible even in discipline.

Back to our opening example: raising a rifle toward our teenager isn't very healthy—it doesn't build self-esteem, it may (if we really stretch it) teach responsibility, and it doesn't exactly promote good Christian fellowship between father and son.

We might be tempted to think that it is impossible to find the "ideal" discipline. A situation comes up, we react, the deed is done, and as the verbal smoke clears, we realize we haven't given much thought to using the discipline as a teaching tool for anything. You're right; perhaps we will seldom use the ideal disciplinary method that fulfills all three purposes. But we can do some thinking and preparing ahead of time and thereby train ourselves to improve. If we understand what's at stake, and have been using a method that tears down, we can learn that there are *better options*.

Discipline methods that accomplish the three goals of building self-esteem, responsibility, and the family as a Christian support group are *always* better than those that don't. Discipline methods that destroy self-esteem, teach nothing about responsibility, and hurt the family esprit de corps are *never* appropriate, even if they seem to "work" in the short run. Our job as parents is to retrain ourselves, by God's grace and strength, to use better, more Kingdom-productive options. Now let's look at the eighteen methods.

1. Bible Study/Memorization

This is a unique method of discipline used by some Christian parents where the parent requires the young person to memorize or study a passage of Scripture appropriate to the offense (e.g., lying, stealing, etc.) or to the subject of obedience. Depending on how it is administered, the method could teach responsibility. Using Scripture as a punishment, however, is probably more likely to turn a kid off to Scripture than anything else.

2. Bribery

Here the parent basically pays the young person to stop misbehaving or to be good. An obvious example at a younger age would be the parent who promises a child a lollipop if she will stop screaming in the supermarket. What the child learns is that if you want a lollipop—*scream*. At an older age the payoff may be in cash or other material goods, but it is directly linked to a specific behavior. This is in contrast to Positive Rewards (to be described later), which reinforces growth—a dynamic that reflects real life.

In theory, Bribery might build a perverse kind of self-esteem as the young person discovers how to work the family system for material gain, but we don't really want to develop such manipulative skills in our children, and there are certainly better values to teach than materialism.

3. Community Service

This method links a poor choice requiring discipline with work or service done in behalf of others outside the home. It could be raking leaves for an elderly neighbor, going with the parent to help at a soup kitchen for the poor, or volunteering to assist the janitor or secretary at church.

This is a positive method in that, though the young person may not be that thrilled initially about having to do this work, he or she is likely to get grateful affirmation from whomever is being helped by the work being done. It is one of the few discipline methods that builds self-esteem. It can teach responsibility. On the down side, Community Service with an eleven- to thirteen-year-old may require a parent's time also—though it could turn into a wonderful "together time" for both parent and young person, and build Christian support within the family.

4. Contracting

We know as parents that contracts contain many features, spelling out the duties and obligations of both signing parties. Similarly, Contracting, when used as discipline or to prevent misbehavior, contains several features. Fitzhugh Dodson was one of the first to recommend this as a method of discipline. In his book *How to Discipline with Love*, he spells out several important features:[1]

- It is mutual agreement negotiated between the parent(s) and the young person. A parent saying, "You will mow the lawn, and I will let you use the car" is not using Contracting. It was not a mutual agreement, it was not negotiated.
- It is written down and signed by both parties.

- It is specific, leaving no room for ambiguity. "If Joe is more respectful of his mother, he will get to stay out later on weekends" is not specific enough. What does it mean to "be more respectful"? What specific behaviors would the parents need to see that demonstrate respect? What does it mean to "stay out later"? The parent and young person might have very different opinions as to what those words mean.

- Things should be stated positively, not negatively. "If John doesn't clean the bathroom on Tuesdays and Fridays he will not receive his ten dollars per week allowance" is specific but negative. Rather say: "Upon successful cleaning of the bathroom on Tuesdays and Fridays, John will be paid ten dollars by his father."

- It must be fair. Both parents and young person must feel as if they are gaining something in the deal. John will probably not enjoy cleaning the bathroom (who really does?) but he does enjoy having ten dollars per week spending money. On the other hand, forty bucks a month for allowance might squeeze the parents' budget, but to not have to do that unpleasant twice-weekly chore is worth something.

- Payoffs should be made only after the task is completed. Also, we should not put our kids down for grumbling as they are in the process of completing their end of the contract. Just how much fun is it really to load the dishwasher or clean up after the family dog? We need to give them freedom to express their feelings. We might just say, "You're right, that isn't any fun, is it?" But if they complete the task, we must make sure we live up to our end of the deal. Fulfilling the contract can teach responsibility, build self-esteem, and the process of negotiating can be a positive family experience.[2]

5. Cut in Allowance

In this approach a specific bad choice on the part of the young person results in less money for allowance. It doesn't exactly build self-esteem or promote the family as a Chris-

tian support group. Since we want, as parents, to teach our
kids good money management, it does the opposite of
teaching them to be responsible. Also, this method is often
misapplied. A kid talks back to us in a mean way and we cut
the allowance. Does that make sense logically?

6. Family Council

This is a regularly scheduled family meeting where issues
are raised and problems worked out among family members.[3] In the family that is a Christian support group it is an
ideal time for sharing hurts, needs, and prayer requests.
With respect to discipline, the Family Council is a time when
an issue can be raised and the wrong behavior discussed. It
would also be a time for appropriate further discipline, or
corrective action could be agreed upon. Christian parents
who use this method successfully give the agenda some
careful thought beforehand. In some families the role of
moderator is rotated. This method can succeed well in all
three purposes of discipline.

7. Forced Apologies

Not much explanation is needed here. "Sara, now you
apologize to your brother for feeding his fish to the cat!"
Repentance must come from the heart for it to do either party
any good. Requiring an apology from someone who doesn't
understand why he or she should make one or doesn't want
to make one only proves who has enough power to make the
requirement. It is the opposite of the Family Council in terms
of meeting our three goals. It may occasionally "work," but
it sure does not accomplish the positive teaching we are
trying to achieve in discipline.

8. Ignoring/Silent Treatment

This is a method in which the parent withholds nurturing
behavior as a punishment for wrongdoing. Not speaking
and not supporting are both examples of this approach. Of
course, one would expect parents whose style is permissive

or ignoring to gravitate in this direction more so than other parents. The survey didn't measure a cousin of this method of discipline: pouting on the part of the parents. Pouting is probably much more widespread.

These methods accomplish nothing positive, with one possible exception. If a young person is evidencing poor social behavior, like nagging or being sarcastic, we can announce our intention to ignore his or her requests when they do so. However, in the remainder of this book, ignoring is meant to be taken in the negative way.

9. Lecturing

This tried-and-true method seems to be the discipline of first recourse in many homes. But a lecture is most successful if it is geared to explanation rather than making the young person feel humiliated. Focusing on blame will be unproductive. Also, the explanation needs to be appropriate for the young person's age. "If you don't do well in school, you won't be able to go to a good college or have a good career" could be true. However, its chance of motivating a seventh-grader is slim. A few thirteen-year-olds may be advanced enough mentally to comprehend it and change their actions, but not many.

Lectures don't build self-esteem unless filled with love and affirmation as well. A lecture has potential to teach responsibility. But if a lecture is really a lecture and not a discussion, it won't do much to promote the family as Christian support group.

10. Loss of Privileges

Here a parent takes away a privilege the young person enjoys. It could be staying up till a certain hour, having use of the car, making decisions about money, having a bedroom phone—all privileges that can be removed appropriately as a discipline method. Usually the lost privilege can be restored after a certain amount of time has elapsed, assuming compliance has been achieved. This method tends to be more positive than its cousin, Restriction. A parent is more likely to say, "Well, I'm sorry you got your third speeding ticket. I'm afraid you've lost the use of the family car." Lost privilege can teach responsibility if handled well.

11. More Chores/Work

Who, as a parent, hasn't given a young person more work as a discipline? Most have. Kids don't usually like it, but it does allow them to work off their guilt if they feel any. A parent can be very affirming if the young person does the job well, and this promotes a good self-image. The method can also teach responsibility if handled properly.

12. Parental Strike

This unusual method is one in which the parent or parents discontinue a provided service, such as meal preparation, laundry service, or some other valued activity. In doing so the parent is trying, in rather dramatic fashion, to gain the attention of the young person who is in need of discipline. It is a way of communicating: "You think the world owes you everything. Well, it doesn't, and in the real world you need to do your share to get along."

The method definitely has potential to build responsibility. However, we'd better think this one through before we attempt it. It's crucial that any service withheld be one that the son or daughter will really miss—and one that the parent is willing to follow through on. "I will no longer clean the house" is likely to meet the limit of the parent's tolerance long before it has a positive effect on a messy teenager. Also, we must clearly spell out why we are going on strike and what behavior needs to be changed before the strike will end. The survey revealed that the Parental Strike was relatively unsuccessful compared to other disciplines. And it won't succeed if the parent is not willing to follow through.

13. Positive Rewards

Here we are not talking about bribery but rewards of affirmation, nurture, and love. Yes, the rewards can be material in nature, but the point is not the "thing"; it's the affirmation for good behavior or good character traits. "Catch someone doing something good, and praise them for it" is one of the axioms of *The One Minute Manager*.[4] I would add: "Catch a teenager showing a good character trait, and praise him for it."

What motivates us as adults? Does an intimidating and power-wielding boss have our respect? We may "obey," but we'd much prefer to work for someone who knows how to manage people well—someone who encourages us, who cares about us individuals, who takes time to get to know us. It's the same way in the home. Positive words and acts of kindness can speak loudly the language of love.

Positive Rewards is a kind of preventative discipline method. We affirm and reward the good behavior or characteristic in hopes of seeing it increase in frequency. Seen any of these in your kids lately? If so, affirm them!

❑ acceptance and love for others
❑ autonomy
❑ determination
❑ good sportsmanship
❑ imagination
❑ initiative
❑ perseverance
❑ respectfulness
❑ responsibility
❑ resourcefulness

A young person would much rather be affirmed than yelled at, so it is a way of relating to our kids that builds their self-esteem, teaches responsibility, and promotes the family as a Christian support group.

It doesn't take too much creativity to think about how to reward the good behavior of our teenagers.

- "Troy, you did a great job on the yard last week, and without even a word of complaint. You're becoming so responsible. I'll do your laundry this week, okay?"

- "Jenny, I really like how you cleaned up the family room after your friends were here the other night. You are so thoughtful, and I appreciate it so much. Here's a gift certificate that'll get you a couple of pizzas at Greasy Joe's. Use 'em sometime when you're out with the gang."
- "Brad, it seems you are really on top of your homework and it makes us so pleased at the good decisions you're making with your time. Let's go out for brunch after church this Sunday. You pick the place."

Positive Rewards don't always need to be given as a surprise. You should also include a positive reward in the Contracting method.

14. Put-downs/Humiliation

"You are so stupid; you're never going to amount to anything!" This is the opposite of Positive Rewards. Here the parent asserts his or her "superiority" over the young person. The discipline may "work" in that the son or daughter is humbled into submission, but the method accomplishes precisely the opposite of what discipline should accomplish. This method is *never* appropriate. The verbal bullets that are fired at our young people will wound them deeply, and it may be years before they recover, if ever.

15. Restriction

This is a common approach linking misbehavior or a bad choice with restricting an activity that the young person wants to do. Most teens dread the words, "You're grounded!" The potential of this negative consequence can teach responsibility as the young person chooses to change his or her behavior. But care must be taken to see that it is really fair (that it's not overreaction to a problem) and enforceable. If you tell a kid he can't drive the car for three weeks when you depend on him to taxi his brothers and sisters to all their activities, *you* may be the one who can't last three weeks. A restriction also works best if it is a logical consequence. The girl who can't manage her phone calls so she can do her homework may have to give up her extension phone until she raises her grades, etc. But restrictions, in and of themselves, do little to promote self-esteem or family unity, so be cautious.

16. Spanking/Hitting

In the ages of eleven to thirteen, Spanking or Hitting was reported as one of the disciplines in 67 percent of the homes. This may seem like a shockingly high statistic, but one can understand why it is used. First of all, it usually "works" because the young person is so humiliated at being treated like a little kid, he or she doesn't want the scene repeated. Second, it is presumed to have a biblical base: "Spare the rod, spoil the child."

We will leave the appropriateness of corporal punishment for younger children to the early-childhood experts, but here it must be said categorically that Spanking or Hitting is *never* appropriate with adolescents. Hitting destroys self-esteem as well as Christian unity in the family. It may teach responsibility, but only in an entirely negative sense, and there are certainly better ways to teach responsibility. On the other hand, it will teach a young person to be devious, to avoid being caught at all costs. The more hurtful the punishment, the more devious the young person is likely to become.[5] There is *always* a better discipline method to use with teenagers than spanking.

Another reason, of course, to stay away from spanking is the danger that it can slide into child abuse. Spanking is so easily done in anger, when the emotions of the parents are out of control. The sad statistics of the extent of this kind of abuse that takes place within Christian homes are becoming widely known.

17. Threatening

This is a clear loser when it comes to any of the three goals we try to accomplish in discipline. It is usually communicated at high volumes. It frequently involves threats that the parents can't, or in a more sober moment realize that they shouldn't, carry out. This only engenders disrespect. It is another method that is *never* appropriate.

18. Yelling

This method is common in many families. To some degree, probably most of us have slipped into it at one time or another. An issue is raised, there's a disagreement, a retort, an accusation, and soon Yelling is used to pummel the other person into submission. Yelling usually means that the situation has gotten out of control. If we want our family to be a Christian support group, building responsibility and self-esteem, Yelling must be taken off our list of discipline methods.

We're not talking here about a loud argument, if that's the cultural style of the family and doesn't involve put-downs, threats, accusations, or other unfair methods that intimidate. In fact there are some families where, in an attempt to be "Christian," all arguments and expressions of anger are taboo. Unfortunately, some children in these families never learn how to handle their negative feelings or resolve differences because they haven't observed the possibility of having a heated disagreement without hurting one another. But Yelling is much more than a loud-but-fair argument. It is the attempt to intimidate by volume.

We've tried to understand what constitutes a good discipline method. Just because it "works" doesn't make it a good one. We've gone through a long list of real discipline methods that are used in Christian families around the country. On the following page, let's try to categorize each method according to what it can produce positively in the lives of our teenagers.

DISCIPLINE METHODS THAT BUILD SELF-ESTEEM

	Always	Probably	Perhaps
Bible Study			✓
Bribery			✓
Community Service		✓	
Contracting		✓	
Family Council		✓	
More Chores			✓
Positive Rewards	✓		

DISCIPLINE METHODS THAT TEACH RESPONSIBILITY

	Always	Probably	Perhaps
Bible Study			✓
Community Service	✓		
Cut in Allowance			✓
Family Council		✓	
Lecturing			✓
Loss of Privileges		✓	
More Chores/Work		✓	
Parental Strike	✓		
Positive Rewards	✓		
Restriction			✓

DISCIPLINE METHODS THAT BUILD UP THE FAMILY AS A CHRISTIAN SUPPORT GROUP

	Always	Probably	Perhaps
Bible Study			✓
Community Service		✓	
Family Council		✓	
Loss of Privileges			✓
Positive Rewards	✓		

It's not hard to notice that some of the eighteen discipline methods do not appear at all on this *positive* list. Things like Spanking/Hitting, Yelling, Threatening, Cut in Allowance, Put-downs/Humiliation, Ignoring/Silent Treatment, and Forced Apologies are all negative in nature. They may be "successful" in that the young person might obey, but they teach nothing positive, and they are always more beneficially replaced by a different method.

Armed with this understanding, let's consider different kinds of kids at different ages. What works, what doesn't? It's no simple subject, that teenager of yours. And to him or her, we devote the next four chapters.

DISCUSSION QUESTIONS

1. Share a recent example of disciplining your son or daughter. Rate the method you used on a scale of 1–5 (5 being best) in terms of accomplishing:

(a) building your son's or daughter's self-esteem;
(b) teaching responsibility;
(c) building your family as a Christian support group.

2. Of the eighteen discipline methods listed, which were your parents' favorites to use on you? Did they "work," that is, did you then obey? What were the positive or negative results of this discipline in your life?

3. As a group, do some brainstorming. Can you think of additional discipline methods to add to your list?

4. Also as a group, see how many positive rewards you can think of that would serve to affirm and encourage your kids.

5. Open your Bible to 2 Timothy 2:24. In what situations in your family do you find it difficult to not be quarrelsome? When are you able to act kindly to all?

SECTION II

WHAT WORKS,
WHAT DOESN'T

5

Ages Eleven to Thirteen
Part I ⎯⎯⎯⎯⎯⎯⎯⎯⎯⎯⎯◇

So what's your kid like, anyway? The years of eleven to thirteen are terrifying and thrilling at the same time for both parent and young person.

As parents we are probably very aware that not all kids are the same. Even when raised in the same family, under very similar conditions, they have different personalities, different ways of relating to their peers and to adults. It's not hard to see how one form of discipline might work well with one kind of young person and be totally ineffective with another type.

Take a few minutes and picture your early adolescent over the last several months. On the following page, check the characteristics that apply at least some of the time.[1] (Later, in Chapters 7 and 8, you'll be able to do the same for your older teenagers.)

No young person will be exclusively one type without any characteristics in the other two columns. Chances are, however, you will find one of these columns to have more items checked than the others. We might conclude that this column is generally descriptive of your eleven- to thirteen-year-old son or daughter.

PERSONALITY CHARACTERISTICS
OF YOUR 11- TO 13-YEAR-OLD

Type 1	Type 2	Type 3
❏ conscientious	❏ avoids conflict	❏ blames others
❏ critical	❏ impatient	❏ charming
❏ list maker	❏ independent	❏ engaging
❏ perfectionist	❏ laid back	❏ good salesperson
❏ reliable	❏ many friends	❏ lies/manipulates
❏ scholarly	❏ mediator	❏ socially mature
❏ serious	❏ rebel	❏ people person
❏ well organized	❏ loyal to peers	❏ shows off
___ Total	___ Total	___Total

Where did the idea to group characteristics in this fashion come from? These are *birth order* characteristics. Type 1 is generally descriptive of first-born children, Type 2 is second-born, and Type 3 is third-born.

Birth order characteristics have received large doses of academic attention in recent years. While there are many exceptions (for example, a second-born might have more first-born characteristics than second-born), kids generally will fall into one of the categories as a most used manner of behavior.

As can be seen in the Appendix, the college-age people who filled out the survey were asked to check the characteristics that they felt generally applied to them. The categories were all merged alphabetically so no grouping (by birth order or anything else) would be obvious. On the second page of the survey, however, they were asked to tell their birth order.

In tabulating the returns, the computer clustered the characteristics as above and correlated them with actual birth order. Sure enough, in most cases people chose the characteristics about themselves that corresponded to their actual birth order. If you are curious about this and want to study the statistics, see the Appendix. See also *The Birth Order Book* by Kevin Leman.[2]

It is crucial that we not get hung up on birth order, though. In this book we are not concerned so much about birth order, but what your young person is actually like. Therefore, in the pages to follow we will refer to Type 1, Type 2, and Type 3 young people, not necessarily to indicate their order of birth but their characteristic type. If Sara is impatient, independent, very loyal to her peer group, and has a tendency to be a rebel, we don't much care what order she was born in relation to her brothers and sisters. The point we will make later is that *her kind of person responds a particular way to certain kinds of discipline.* Some of the eighteen methods of discipline will work better on her than other methods at her age.

If your son or daughter does not neatly fit into one of the types that have been presented, don't worry. There will still be plenty in the pages to follow that will be useful.

Now that you have identified what your son or daughter is generally like, let's get a good grip on what is normal behavior for an early adolescent.

Normal Patterns

Plop yourself down in any seventh-grade classroom in the fall. Most of the kids you see will be twelve.

Take these kids, for example.

- Melissa's twelve going on seventeen, 5'7" tall, 115 pounds, and—depending on her clothes and makeup—she can easily pass for a sixteen-year-old. She is outgoing and very comfortable socially.
- Mark is big for his age too. He's taller than Melissa (most boys in the class aren't), stands erect, and is quite an asset to the junior high basketball team. He is confident, and he certainly notices Melissa.
- Jill's body, on the other hand, doesn't even appear to be getting ready for puberty. She's short, thin, but very, very smart. She is also very, very shy.

- Then there is Bill. He is taller than Jill but looks as if his body were put together by a committee that couldn't agree on much. He's clumsy, kind of a nerd, and has trouble even thinking in complete sentences, let alone being able to write or speak well.

All these kids are completely normal. Why is it vital to understand what is normal? Many parents overdiscipline, reacting to things they see in their young people that are normal and nothing to be concerned about.

Physically

This is the age when most young people experience the onset of puberty. Their hormones begin triggering the physical changes necessary to be parents. Girls generally develop more rapidly than boys. Sexual feelings are awakening in some guys and girls in this awkward stage. Parents will be well advised to remember that young people this age are very aware of the physical changes going on in them—and how they compare with others in this regard.

- *Implications for discipline:* we shouldn't discipline or punish for clumsiness and awkwardness. We should not exert great pressure to be involved in sports or to take leadership roles with their peers. The body might not be ready for the sports, and the self-esteem that comes from a well-developed body will probably be absent if the young person feels his or her physical development is behind the peer group.

Mentally

Most girls and some guys will begin what child developmental psychologist Jean Piaget calls "formal operations." In short, it is the ability to think about a thought. Children can't take a thought and then mentally walk around it, examining it from different angles, wondering why they think that way, or what would be the implications of a different approach. Adults can. With this new ability to test truly *abstract thinking*, the adolescent can begin to reason how a variety of actions in the present might impact the future. This is much more advanced than a fifth-grader who manages to remember (a remarkable accomplishment in itself) that Mom said to get home by six o'clock or miss supper. This new ability allows kids to have thoughts and feelings that are truly their own, distinct and perhaps different from those of their parents. They now question things they once took for granted.

• *Implications for discipline:* Some young people in this age group haven't yet developed the capacity for truly abstract thinking. Therefore, it is useless to threaten them with the loss of a *distant* privilege (summer camp, entrance in college, etc.) as a consequence of present actions. That's too abstract. They need a much more immediate reward or cause and effect. On the other hand, parents should not become alarmed or panicked if, as a kid this age begins to develop independent thinking powers, he or she starts questioning the existence of God or other important truths that were earlier accepted. The questions mean their minds are beginning to develop and absorb facts from all over. They want to make choices based on these facts. They're right on schedule.

Socially

This is a time of great stress socially. Friendship clusters change as kids grow at different rates. Generally the "in crowd" at school and at church are those whose bodies are more physically developed than their peers and those who have begun to have some success in getting along with the opposite sex. It is a time of jostling for position, to gain attention, acceptance, and status.[3] Kids generally want to get along at home, but they also want to please their peers.

• *Implications for discipline:* we can expect that many issues will arise related to our young person's friends and activities with those friends.

Emotionally

This period is an emotional roller coaster. The highs are high and the lows are low. This young person can be loud and rowdy at 9:00 A.M. and quiet and shy by 9:30 A.M. Sometimes they are virtually trying on different personalities, different ways of relating to their world. They're sending out signals and seeing what kind of feedback returns. Insecurity, a poor self-esteem, can show itself through shyness, depression, rowdiness, rudeness, and unkindness. "Imaginary audience behavior"[4] is common. This is where the young person thinks everyone is as aware of his or her behavior and appearance as he or she is. A pimple or hair that doesn't look just right can result in profound depression or withdrawal.

• *Implications for discipline:* Kids this age are extremely susceptible to being hurt by put-downs and criticism. If we use put-downs in trying to influence their behavior, we can almost guarantee we are doing significant damage. Moodiness in our young people is frustrating to us as parents, but we shouldn't be disciplining them for it. We may, however, have to discipline negative behavior (such as yelling or hitting) that stems from moodiness.

Spiritually

This can be a time of deepening faith, depending on our young person's mental development. Kids who are able to think abstractly can grasp a whole new level of meaning from the Gospel and the implications of the Christ-life.

• *Implications for discipline:* We shouldn't panic if twelve-year-old Johnny is not a spiritual giant yet. His thirteen-year-old sister may be, but it could be awhile before he is ready to make a stand for Christ.

"You Mean We're Not the Only Ones?"

If we have had many children and our youngest is now reaching adolescence, we have had lots of experience and need no schooling as to what to expect next. On the other hand, if we are new at facing this stage of family life, we might be quite bewildered by the new issues we are forced to face.

Twelve-year-old William confronts his father as he finishes loading the dishwasher.

"Dad, it's not fair that I'm only allowed to watch the same amount of TV as Jennifer and Tom. They're three years younger than I am. I can stay up later, and I've shown you I know how to get my homework done on time. I deserve better treatment."

What's a parent to say? A "No because I said so" won't exactly foster good communication and will almost certainly ensure another similar confrontation soon. It may not be about television, but it will be about some arena where the young person thinks you are cramping his or her expanding world.

What parents and kids disagree about in the home is another one of those subjects that has drawn the attention of researchers through the years. One major study of seventh-graders and their families found that most disagreements were about personal habits and family obligations, as opposed to problems with peer relations.[5]

That same study listed various "rule situations" within the home and the extent that the parent and young person disagreed. In the chart on the next page, the check marks indicate the major problem areas in the two hundred families studied.[6] (There was *some* conflict in each of the rule situations that are listed in the chart, but only the major ones received a check mark.)

Hopefully, this information reassures you that the conflicts in your home are normal. If your oldest child has not yet reached early adolescence, you may be able to hit these waves on a more even keel, knowing that they aren't unusual.

In families with seventh-graders (particularly some girls) who are a little more advanced, you may already be facing conflicts over dating, going steady, etc. These are situations needing special guidance, and they are discussed in subsequent chapters.

**THE SOURCES OF CONFLICT
FOR FAMILIES WITH SEVENTH-GRADERS**

Rule Situation	Conflict With Son	Conflict With Daughter
Peer Relation		
Time in on weekend		
Amount of dating		
Going steady		
Time with certain guys		
Time with certain girls		
Personal Habits		
Watching TV	✓	✓
Homework	✓	✓
Grooming	✓	
Spending money		
Eating habits	✓	
Clothes		
Family Obligations		
Cleanliness of room	✓	✓
Family activities		
Religious activities		
Helping at home	✓	✓

Normal Parenting

How do most Christian parents deal with their kids, ages eleven to thirteen? My survey introduced the college-age participants to the three parenting styles described in Chapter 3 and asked them to recall their experience during the years of eleven through thirteen and report what style their parents used. Memories are selective, and young people may view their parents' approach as somewhat stricter than it was, but the relationship between the styles is probably accurate. Also, other research confirms that parents and kids generally have the same perception of what parenting style is being or has been used.[7]

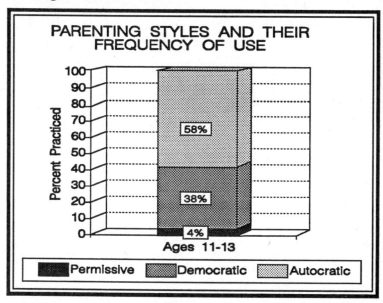

As this graph demonstrates, the authoritarian/autocratic style was the distinct preference in 58 percent of the families while almost no parents (4 percent) used the permissive/ignoring style at this age. Those two facts may result from parents perceiving that they still needed to be in control. As Christians we have expectations, standards, and preferences; we want to be good parents; we want our kids to grow up loving God and evidencing His life in them.

When it came to discipline in the survey, "success" was defined as when the young persons obeyed or accepted the discipline. They may not have liked it, but they obeyed it nonetheless. In the graph on the following page, you can see how the young people perceived the success of the parenting style they lived under at this age.

Generally speaking, the kids obeyed their parents no matter what style was used. It is not hard to understand why. Most kids this age want to please their parents. They understand intuitively that they are *totally* dependent on them. At

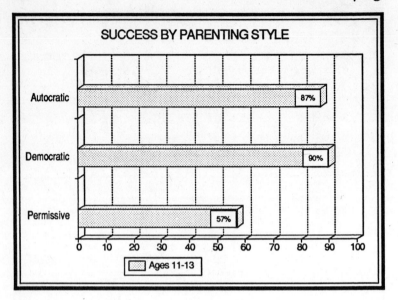

SUCCESS BY PARENTING STYLE

this age young people are still looking to their parents for guidance and help. As you can see, the autocratic/authoritarian style is almost as good as the democratic/equalitarian style, particularly when combined with high nurture.

Some of those who said their parents were autocratic/authoritarian in style, and were successful with discipline, mentioned the love they felt from Mom and Dad.

- An eighteen-year-old female from Washington State noted: "Complete honesty, respect for all authority, loyalty were all emphasized in my family. Forgiveness and unconditional love were also biggies."
- A twenty-two-year-old male from New York said, "Physical punishment worked, but I knew they loved me and forgave me. I wanted to please my parents."

The Christian example of the parents and their relationship to God received some comments from young people whose parents used this style at that age.

- An eighteen-year-old from Minnesota shared: "I believe it was their faith in the Lord [that made them successful at discipline]. They trusted in Jesus to help make all their decisions and they used Him as a guideline. Our family life was centered around the Lord."

Love and support were mentioned far more, however, by young people whose parents used the democratic/equalitarian style.

- A twenty-year-old from California reported: "When they were successful it was usually due to the fact that they did it in a very loving way . . . one that I could see and understand."

So what is normal? In nearly six out of ten families, the authoritarian/autocratic style was used and was generally successful—over 87 percent of the time. In almost four out of ten families, the democratic/equalitarian style was used with this age son or daughter and was successful about 90 percent of the time.

In Chapter 3, I claimed that the democratic/equalitarian approach was the best "style for smiles," but it might not be for this age young person—it all depends on his or her mental development.

The democratic/equalitarian approach is best when a young person's mind has matured to the "think about a thought" stage. The young person won't make good decisions if he or she can't understand the consequences of a decision. When early adolescents are able to think through the choices that face them and the consequences they may lead to, they will respond best to the democratic/equalitarian style.

On the flip side, a young person who cannot think abstractly is more likely to respond well to an authoritarian parent, especially if there is high nurturing and no abuse. His mind does not freely explore the options that the parent did not offer or discuss with him. He doesn't sit and think, "Well, Mom wants 'A,' but I could do 'B' or 'C' or 'D' instead." Many kids this age, especially boys, don't think that options B, C, or D even exist.

A wise parent will change the parenting style to democratic/equalitarian as the young person's mental development matures.

Take a moment and think about what kind of parenting you are using with your early adolescent. How do you feel things are going? Does your son or daughter still need direct guidance, or is he or she beginning to have the mental equipment to make independent decisions?

DISCUSSION QUESTIONS

1. Try to remember back to seventh grade. Describe yourself briefly in each of the areas considered in this chapter:

- Physically
- Mentally
- Socially
- Emotionally
- Spiritually

2. Briefly describe your own eleven- to thirteen-year-old in terms of these same characteristics.

3. What personality "type" (1, 2, or 3) is your young adolescent?

4. Look at the chart on page 78 titled, "The Sources of Conflict for Families With Seventh-Graders." In what areas are you now having conflict with your young teen?

5. Open your Bible to 1 Corinthians 13:4–7. Which of these characteristics of love do you feel operate best in your home? Which do you feel need the most improvement?

6

Ages Eleven to Thirteen
Part II _____ ◆

It's a nice, relaxing weekend at home. You and your two adolescents, ages eleven and thirteen, have gotten along pretty well. All members of the family have been free to do their own thing. However, your kids know that one of their chores, to be done before Sunday supper, is to clean their rooms. They also know that there will be some kind of discipline if they don't. You have politely reminded them on two occasions about their responsibility to complete this chore. Each time they cheerfully assured you that it would be done—not now, but "Don't worry, it will get done in plenty of time."

Sunday comes. Supper is at 5:00 P.M.; it's now 4:55. You take a walk down the hall and two open doors confirm your fears: both rooms look as if wild animals had been trapped inside for a week. Your kids are nowhere to be seen. You walk back down the hall, down to the basement, and as you approach the family room you hear them playing the latest Nintendo game.

In this situation you . . .

What Discipline Methods Do You Use?

When faced with a discipline situation, each of us tends to have a repertoire of methods that we draw upon. Take a few moments and consider which methods you use with your kids, ages eleven to thirteen. If you need further explanation go back to Chapter 4. Place a check corresponding to the methods you are using; circle those you consider successful.

Method	Youth #1	Youth #2
DISCIPLINE METHODS USED WITH YOUR 11- TO 13-YEAR-OLD		
1. Bible Study/ Memorization		
2. Bribery		
3. Community Service		
4. Contracting		
5. Cut in Allowance		
6. Family Council		
7. Forced Apologies		
8. Ignoring/ Silent Treatment		
9. Lecturing		
10. Loss of Privileges		
11. More Chores/Work		

Method	Youth #1	Youth #2
12. Parental Strike		
13. Positive Rewards		
14. Put-downs/ Humiliation		
15. Restriction		
16. Spanking/ Hitting		
17. Threatening		
18. Yelling		
19. Other		

List here the three discipline methods you use most often that you feel are working well—that is, that your kids seem to obey.

	Youth #1	Youth #2
Method One:	_____	_____
Method Two:	_____	_____
Method Three:	_____	_____

What Works, What Doesn't?

What works and what doesn't for you? If you've filled out the above questionnaire, you have a feel for that. Now, let's compare your answers to what worked with our 385 college-age young people as they looked back at their own early adolescence. In the last chapter we looked at success in terms of *parenting style*. This time we are looking at success in terms of specific *disciplinary methods*. Remember, we are not evaluating the merits of the method in terms of building self-esteem, etc., just what was "effective" in terms of securing your teen's obedience. The list is ranked in terms of that effectiveness.

DISCIPLINE METHODS
RANKED BY "EFFECTIVENESS"
AGES 11 TO 13

Discipline Method	Percent Families Where Used	Percent Effective
1. Positive Rewards	64	93
2. Loss of Privileges	65	92
3. Spanking/Hitting	66	87
4. Restriction	60	87
5. Family Council	28	84
6. Cut in Allowance	21	81
7. More Chores/Work	42	80
8. Lecturing	78	80
9. Bible Study/Memorization	16	73
10. Contracting	10	67
11. Community Service	9	57
12. Threatening	44	55
13. Bribery	12	53
14. Yelling	66	48
15. Parental Strike	11	47
16. Forced Apologies	32	45
17. Ignoring	21	35
18. Put-downs/Humiliation	27	29

A variety of observations can be made as we ponder this long list. Only five of the eighteen methods fail to "work" with this age group at least half the time. On the other hand, consider what else this list can tell us.

What Not to Use and Why

If we're shopping for successful discipline methods to use on young people ages eleven to thirteen, we will probably reject Put-downs/Humiliation, Ignoring, Forced Apologies, Yelling, and a Parental Strike! Unfortunately Yelling is used in two-thirds of all families, Forced Apologies in nearly one-third, and Put-downs/Humiliation occur in one-fourth of all families. As mentioned before, Yelling, Forced Apologies, and Put-downs/Humiliation all serve to escalate the tension in the home. They block effective communication. Yelling and Put-downs/Humiliation destroy a young person's self-esteem, and they fail to bring the family together as a Christian support group.

Why do we as parents use these methods? Perhaps it is all we had modeled to us when we were young. Perhaps we face so much stress through our workday that we have no reserves of patience left for our kids. Or maybe we just need to admit we're imperfect parents with imperfect personalities who very much need the grace of God and the presence of Christ in our lives to work a change in our hearts.

We might wonder why the Parental Strike was not more effective. The survey showed that this method was similarly unsuccessful with both middle and late adolescents. To work right, a Parental Strike has to be done properly and with adequate advance notice.[1] Many parents may threaten a Parental Strike or a version thereof but don't really follow through. This can be an effective discipline method, but the *parent* needs to be strong willed enough to follow through.

What to Use and Why

Let's look at the top end of the list. Positive rewards come out as the most effective motivator of good behavior in a young person this age. It is not hard to understand why it works. Even adults are more strongly motivated by love, encouragement, thankfulness, and praise—not anger and threats.

That Loss of Privileges and Restriction rank in the top four should come as no surprise either. Early-adolescent young people are beginning to feel the desire for independence and self-expression. As their mental horizons begin to expand, so does their desire for more freedom. It makes them feel grown up to stay up later at night, to manage their own money, to take the bus to the mall with a friend, and choose their own clothing. All of these things are rites of passage that signal "you're getting older." Take those away, and it's back to being a baby again. We can be certain that only rarely will a person this age want to be younger rather than older. These two discipline methods don't build self-esteem in and of themselves, but they can teach responsibility. And once responsibility is achieved, that brings a good sense of self-esteem.

We might be surprised to see that Spanking and Hitting ranks in the top four successful methods with this age group. It was used in two-thirds of the homes represented in the survey. It works with this age group for the same reason Restriction and Loss of Privileges work—whether it hurts or not, spanking means you're being treated like a baby. Kids this age don't want to be treated like babies, and spanking as a discipline denies them the respect they want (and need) as maturing young people.

Of course, spanking or hitting can hurt, too, and most young people would rather not be hurt. Spanking may still be popular among parents because it "gets results" and requires no great amount of thought or consideration. It may be a tempting selection from the menu, but there is *always* a better method!

Remember Type 1, Type 2, and Type 3 characteristics for young people (Chapter 5)? The discipline methods that ranked as the top four apply fairly consistently within each type of young person this age. (See the chart on the following page.) Over 42 percent indicated they generally evidenced Type 1 characteristics, just over 41 percent indicated Type 2, and over 8 percent indicated Type 3.

It is fascinating to note that the top four discipline methods with both the Type 1 and Type 3 young people include the same four methods as the general rankings on page 86. The order is slightly different, but the percentages (see the

---

**TOP FOUR EFFECTIVE DISCIPLINE METHODS
BY TYPE OF YOUNG PERSON, AGES 11 TO 13**

Type 1	Type 2	Type 3
Loss of Privileges	Positive Rewards	Spanking
Positive Rewards	Loss of Privileges	Positive Rewards
Spanking	Cut in Allowance	Loss of Privileges
Restriction	Restriction	Restriction

Appendix) are all in the high 80s to mid 90s. A reason Spanking might be highest on the Type 3 list is that Type 3 young people have a tendency to be the family clown. Their behaviors can be seen as irresponsible and become exasperating to the parents. Spanking may seem to get the message across better if the kid needs to settle down. However, before you elevate Spanking to your number-one disciplinary method with your Type 3 adolescent, remember that it fails miserably to achieve any of the three goals for good discipline: it does not build self-esteem, responsibility, or the family as a Christian support group.

We will notice that Type 2 young people have a somewhat different list. Spanking drops off the list. Type 2 kids have a high potential for independence, stubbornness, and having a rebellious spirit. They are likely to think, if not say out loud: "Go ahead and spank, I don't care. I'm not going to change and there is nothing you can do to make me!"

On the other hand, cutting their allowance is a high motivator because money means independence to Type 2 adolescents, and they are very peer-oriented. They are aware of fashion, being "in," and having all the right things. Money is the key to having things and Type 2 young people will be highly motivated to maintain their source of income.

We might wonder if guys and girls differ in their response to certain methods of discipline at this age. There was no difference among the top four most successful methods comparing guys to girls. The order was slightly different, but not significantly so. However, further down the list there were some notable differences.

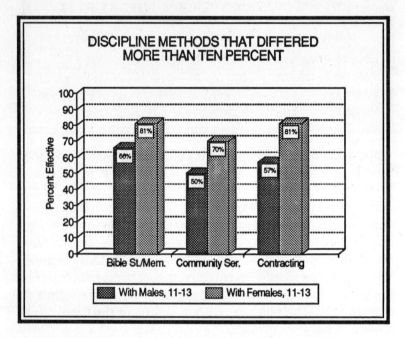

These differences can be easily accounted for because girls in this age group are more mature mentally than their male counterparts. They are more able to grasp the longer-term implications of their actions. They are able to connect the discipline with their bad choice and adjust their behavior accordingly.

Need a Better Option?

On page 85 you were asked to list your top three discipline methods. Do you recall what parenting style you chose in Chapter 3?

The nearly 400 college-age young people reported their parents' top three discipline methods by parenting style at this age as follows:

<u>Autocratic/Authoritarian</u>
    Lecture
    Spanking
    Yelling

<u>Democratic/Equalitarian</u>
    Lecture
    Positive Rewards
    Loss of Privileges

<u>Permissive/Ignoring</u>
    Positive Rewards
    Lecture
    Yelling

How should you evaluate your top three choices? If you go just by what "works," or what is common in other homes, you may "succeed" at achieving compliance from your sons and daughters. However, if the methods you are using are negative in nature, you will miss many teaching opportunities and you may alienate your young people. Look back through the list of eighteen discipline methods and think again about what will produce something positive in their lives. Learn to always think in terms of building self-esteem, building responsibility, and building the family as a Christian support group.

If change seems necessary, how will you accomplish it? It will take some conscious effort, but it can be done. Try these steps:

Step 1

Recall your top three most-used discipline methods. List them on the left and whatever better options you can think of on the right—if you think change is necessary.

<u>Most Used Methods</u>	<u>Better Choices</u>
1. _____	_____
2. _____	_____
3. _____	_____

Step 2

Commit your desire to change for the better to the Lord in prayer. Agree on this with your spouse; share it with your closest Christian friends or support group.

Step 3

Apologize to your son or daughter if you have been using a negative approach. Ask them to pray for you about this. You'll have their attention—guaranteed. Tell them also that they have your permission to politely call it to your attention if you slip back into a negative discipline method.

Step 4

With your spouse or close Christian friend, recall the most recent examples in your family where negative discipline methods were used. Role-play, or at least talk through in detail, how a *better option* could have been used.

Step 5

In the next circumstance requiring discipline, try the new method you have decided upon. Some time afterward, perhaps a few days, ask your son or daughter how they felt, compared with what you usually might have done.

It is obvious that we are trying to not only change our discipline methods but also to establish communication links with our young person.

Many of the young people who filled out the survey commented on specific kinds of discipline or the importance of how it is carried out.

- An eighteen-year-old female from New York said, "Parents should discipline their child without the anger of the moment and look for the type of discipline most fitting."
- A seventeen-year-old male from New York commented: "Always be sure to remember that there are two sides to each story, that your kids are people, too, and be respectful of their rights as human beings, i.e., don't be cruel or excessively manipulative. Also, always make your child well aware that you discipline out of love."

- One twenty-one-year-old female from Washington State added: "Start young. Don't start trying to discipline when they're teenagers; it's too late then. Allow them input, and give them some of their own things to make decisions about. Most of all, be their friend. Spend time with them, not talking about school or household chores but what's gone on in their lives . . . what's important to them. Be a friend to them and be encouraging of openness. A friendship with a teen is the most valuable leverage a parent can have. It not only tells the teen they can come to you to talk about anything, it can give them a sense of self-worth, that you found them worthwhile enough to establish such an intimate relationship with them that's beyond parent/ child."

Meanwhile, Back in the Family Room

As this chapter opened you were asked to picture yourself having discovered that your eleven- and thirteen-year-olds had not cleaned their rooms by Sunday 5:00 P.M., as requested. You walked down the hall toward the family room and heard the sounds of the latest video game as well as your kids commenting on the electronic battle they were engaged in.

Your standard reaction would be . . . yelling? Would you threaten? Would you criticize their irresponsibility? How about this:

Mr. Mills enters the family room quietly. His kids are so engaged in their game that they don't even notice he's in the room. Before he even opens his mouth he breathes a prayer of thanks for his children and for his desire to not mess up this teaching opportunity.

"Jim, Emily, is your game about done?"

"About a minute, okay?"

"Sure, I'll just watch."

Dad continues. "That looks like fun. I'd like to play that sometime, but now it's time for supper. Say, can either of you remember anything you may have forgotten to do this weekend?"

"No, Dad, what?" eleven-year-old Jim replies.

"Oh my gosh, our rooms," Emily gasps.

Dad smiles. "Yep, it's five o'clock Sunday night, and I'm afraid time's out. Neither room is done, and I did remind you both, twice."

"We're really sorry!"

"So am I, kids, so am I. Your mom and I have talked about it and we'd like to give you each a choice about the discipline you'll receive. You both have to clean your room before you get supper tonight, but between now and Monday bedtime you need to do one of the following:

"Jim, you can either bring the next week's wood for the wood stove into the garage—about a third of a cord, I'd say—or you can go next door and rake Mrs. Miller's leaves.

"Emily, you can either do the laundry when you get home from school tomorrow or you can help me at church tomorrow night. It's our turn to clean the nursery and fellowship hall.

"Next weekend, of course, you'll need to clean your room by five on Sunday, as usual. If you fail, you can choose two of three options, instead of one out of two like tonight.

"You may wonder why it's important to your mom and me to have your rooms look decent at least once a week. You both get really frustrated when you can't find stuff, and when things are clean it's easier to find. You come to your mom and me to ask for help, but we sure don't know where things are in that mess. You do yourself a big favor by being a little more organized. Sure, it's work, but it saves time in the end, and I know you're both capable. There are other reasons, too, but that's the main one right now."

The approach Mr. Mills has taken has been pretty positive. He managed to break from his normal yelling to a much more Spirit-controlled manner—calmly talking with the kids. He has given the kids options, affirming their own decision-making ability. Some options are Community Service in nature and hold the possibility for substantial affirmation for the kids from others. The other options at least set up the possibility of Dad or Mom affirming them.

In addition, Mr. Mills may use a Positive Reward if they get their rooms clean on time the following Sunday. (Ice cream sundaes make great Positive Rewards.)

Next weekend he will gently remind his semi-airhead (though very normal) son what was just discussed. He knows his daughter well enough to know that she'll remember and have no problem completing the task.

The disciplines chosen by Jim and Emily to be completed before Monday bedtime will require varying degrees of parental supervision and follow-through. He and his wife have already decided who will oversee what.

Does his approach have a good chance for success? No plan is foolproof, but this approach stands a good chance of teaching responsibility, building self-esteem, and helping their family as a Christian unit.

We've considered what's normal in early adolescence and how various kinds of discipline work. If you have or are about to have a child in this age group in your home, you may need to reflect for a while on what has been said and whether you want to develop any new methods of discipline. The discussion questions will assist your reflection. Next we take a look at the middle adolescent: ages fourteen through sixteen.

DISCUSSION QUESTIONS

1. Which were the favorite discipline methods your parents used on you when you were eleven through thirteen?

2. What did they have to discipline you about? How did you respond?

3. What are the top three methods you are using on your

young person? How successful are those methods? Do you need a more positive option? If so, which do you think might work in your situation?

4. This question will require considerable openness and vulnerability on your part. Open your Bible to Hebrews 12:7–12. How have you been disciplined by the Lord? How did it feel? Has your behavior changed?

7

Ages Fourteen
To Sixteen ———————

Phil and Lynn Jones have spent an enjoyable evening with
friends. They laughed, played Pictionary, and now as they
clean up the dishes together, they feel a deep satisfaction
about their lives and the family God has given them.

David, their sixteen-year-old, is out for the evening. They
asked him to be home by midnight on this Saturday night,
as they plan to attend early service at church in the morning.

Phil and Lynn are in bed by 11:30. In only a few minutes
Phil is thoroughly sleeping. Lynn, however, lies awake.
David has only had his license for six months and she never
really relaxes enough to fall asleep until she hears him open
the garage door. Midnight comes . . . then 12:15, 12:30, 12:45.
Lynn is wide awake now and very tense. It's 1:00 A.M.

"Dear?"

Phil jerks in surprise. "Wha . . . what? What's wrong?
What time is it?"

"David's not home, and it's one o'clock."

Together they pray for his safety and about their reaction
when he does come home. Soon 1:15 arrives, then 1:30.
Finally at 1:45 they hear the garage door open.

What to do now?

Middle adolescence is a time of new challenges in our role as parents. The world of our sons and daughters has expanded tremendously. With their increased desire for independence comes an increasing challenge in many families to continue to guide their young people. When we think about the subject of discipline and our kids fourteen to sixteen, it will help us first of all to realize what "normal" teenagers are like at this stage.

Normal Patterns

Physically

In these years the adolescent body begins to even out. By age sixteen, the major growth spurt is about over, clumsiness subsides, and most males are pleased to once again be taller than most females. If the young person is athletically inclined, there is immense potential for using his or her growing body to its fullest. As with their early-adolescent counterparts, teenagers in this group are aware of how they compare physically with their peers. The subject of sex and the female body as a sexual object becomes a matter of intense interest and preoccupation to most males in these years. Many girls (and even some adult women) are unaware of how intense this obsession is, while a few have already learned how to exploit it.

Mentally

Most guys catch up to the girls in the ability to think abstractly, and for both sexes whole new mental horizons have suddenly burst upon their consciousness. They *can* think and (believe it or not) think before they act. They can ponder an action and mentally measure its projected result as well as the wider consequences of that result.

It is a time of life when kids begin to think about where they are going, what they will do after high school. Childhood is gone; there's no turning back, and they can begin to see themselves in the future. Tony Campolo, nationally known Christian sociologist, affirms, "The more real the future is to people, the more they'll be willing to make present sacrifices to enjoy future rewards . . . young people will make the sacrifice in time and energy to do well in school if they can picture the benefits they'll enjoy years later as a result of a good education."[1]

All this mental work going on inside the head of the average fourteen- to sixteen-year-old means that he or she is also forming independent opinions about many matters. Most will be very frustrated if they are not allowed to express these opinions when it becomes obvious that the parents' ideas are different from theirs.

• *Implications for discipline:* An autocratic or authoritarian approach will begin to result, not in unquestioned obedience, but in tension, argument, and stress. The survey results show that the success of this approach drops by nearly half compared to the early-adolescent stage. Teenagers need to feel their ideas are important; they need choices, respect, and to be listened to. Parents who don't learn to give their kids some room to make their own choices in this period drive their kids away from themselves and toward their peers

Socially

Whereas the earlier stage could be described as jostling, the stage of middle adolescence can be described as settling in to a subset of their peer group.[2] If we take the roof off our local high school, we will notice immediately that middle-adolescent society has divided itself into several subgroups. We'll notice the rebels smoking out at the edge of the parking lot, the musicians and artists congregating in the lunchroom, the jocks and their admirers swaggering down the halls. The preppies will be out on the lawn catching a few rays, while the leaders of student government gravitate around the Activities Coordinator's office. And of course there are the nerds, hanging out in the computer room or rewiring the whole school's sound system. Yes, there is some mixing, but generally a young person has made his or her friendship choices before this period is over.

Another important feature is that socializing becomes one of the young person's highest priorities. It is a time to figure out how to relate to the opposite sex. First exchanges take place during the school day, then carry over to afterschool activities. Group dating will be done by many and single dating by some as the sixteenth year concludes.

• *Implications for discipline:* We can expect, as parents, to have to deal with a host of issues related to the need our kids have to be out with their peers. Much more on this later.

Emotionally

Because of what has happened in their mental development, most young people of this age are capable of caring and empathy. They can begin to understand our point of view as parents if we take care in how we explain it, and they can care deeply about other people. The highs are still pretty high and the tragedies still pretty tragic, yet these young people will make progress in dealing with the experiences that come their direction. They are learning to integrate their experiences and their own feelings into some kind of consistent pattern of behavior.

• *Implications for discipline:* This emotional development combined with the mental development gives many young people this age the ability to be reasonable when it comes to rules, consequences, and responsibility. On the other hand, the rules need to make sense to them and reassure them that they truly are on a path of gradual emancipation.

Spiritually

Since their mental development has paved the way for understanding consequences, the Gospel can take on a new and deeper meaning at this age. They understand that being a Christian should make a difference in terms of how they actually live. They are capable of connecting the fact that wanting to please God should have some impact on how they behave at home and with us as their parents. From ages fourteen to sixteen is a time when the Christian young person may "rededicate" his or her life to Christ and begin to have joy in serving Him.

• *Implications for discipline:* If the parents are sincerely trying to help the family become a Christian community, the young person who is growing as a Christian will be responsive, at least some of the time. If the parents are able to come across as "fellow strugglers" in this thing called life, strong ties can be forged between parent and teenager. Kids can grasp how their actions hurt them spiritually as well as hurt the unity they have in the family. Some of the survey respondents commented on this connection when asked why their parents were successful with discipline.

- A twenty-one-year-old male from Georgia said, "I was a good Christian and generally needed little discipline."
- An eighteen-year-old male from Minnesota added: "When I rededicated my life to Christ I wanted to obey [my parents] . . . my parents loved God and me."

Normal Issues

We saw that in the previous stage much of the discipline issues had to do with personal habits, such as TV watching, grooming, etc. Now the issues for potential problems expand beyond these concerns.

Chores

Most parents expect their middle-adolescent young people to contribute to the work necessary to keep the household functioning. Of course many children and early adolescents have chores, too, but in this stage chore expectations are present in nearly all families. In a survey of over 150,000 teenagers, Norman and Harris discovered what kinds of chores guys and girls at this age were expected to do by their parents.[3]

COMMON CHORES FOR MIDDLE TEENS

Chores Expected	Percent Girls	Percent Boys
Make bed	76	55
Do dishes	61	24
Clean house	49	24
Baby-sit	41	22
Cook	36	14
Do laundry	35	12
Take out garbage	48	65
Yard work	31	50
Wash car	30	38
Paint or make repairs	13	34

It's not hard to see that the top half of the list shows more female-oriented chores and the bottom half shows more male-oriented ones.

Curfew

As kids want to spend time with their peers outside the normal school day, most families begin to deal with just how much time is allowed, and especially what time to be home at night. Some parents, with their kids already behaving quite responsibly, see no need to set limits or are able to work them out amicably on a case-by-case basis. In other cases, limits may need to be set, though it is much better to negotiate the curfew with the young person instead of imposing it without discussion.

Letting the teenager become involved in the decision-making process increases the likelihood of the decision being followed.[4]

Calling Home

If this is important to you as a parent, you need to model it. If Dad or Mom gets delayed at the office, it's important to call home and let people know. If the teenager sees it as "courteous family policy," it will not be resented as an invasion of privacy.[5]

Driving and Riding

During most of this age period our kids will be riders, not drivers. One fascinating study was done which asked nearly 19,000 teenagers about their parents' rules when it came to riding in the cars of others. Compare this with your own expectations.

PARENTAL RESTRICTIONS ON TEEN TRAVEL AS A PASSENGER[6]

Type of Restriction	Parents Don't Care	Implicitly Expected	Explicitly Required
Not travel with drivers who drink	6%	29%	66%
Tell them where I'm going	7	29	64
Be home by a certain time	11	31	58
Not go without their permission	14	34	51
Tell them who is driving	18	36	47
Not go with drivers they don't know	23	34	42
Not travel with certain drivers	27	36	38
Not go in bad weather	49	35	16

Whether it is driving, riding, curfew, or whatever, there are bound to be occasional differences between parents and kids.

In trying to understand what is normal in families during this age period, we've looked at normal adolescent development and some of the normal issues that arise. Let's also look at what is normal in parenting styles.

Normal Parenting

How do most Christian parents deal with their kids, ages fourteen to sixteen? Our survey showed a definite shift in style from what was used at an earlier age.

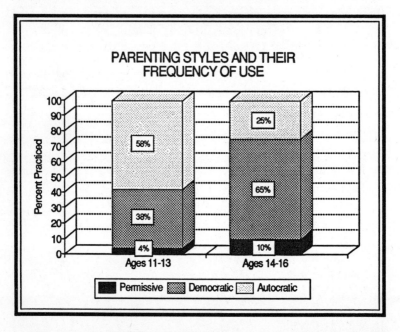

What a change! The number of those using the autocratic approach is less than half of what it was a few years ago, and those using both the democratic and permissive approaches have nearly doubled, with the democratic approach being the favorite.

On the following page you can see how successful the discipline was perceived to be by the young people, according to the style of parenting used at this age.

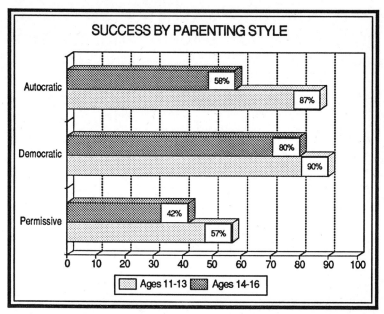

Once again the democratic/equalitarian style is the most successful of the three, but this time dramatically more successful than the autocratic/authoritarian style. If you find yourself staring at this chart and realizing you're not using a successful style, take heart; Chapter 10 will suggest how to make positive changes in your parenting style.

The Norman/Harris study that reported the most common chores for 150,000 middle teens also affirms this conclusion and helps parents understand how the democratic/equalitarian approach can operate when setting guidelines and limits. The study asserts that . . .

- Rules must be realistic.
- We must warn about consequences of an action.
- We must listen to explanations.[7]

It is especially in listening that we show our respect for the thinking ability and opinions of our teenagers.

Armed with all this understanding about what is normal, let's now turn our attention to your kids and the discipline methods you use.

Your Middle Adolescent and the Disciplines You Use

Take a moment and consider your teenager. Check the characteristics you have seen as generally true about your son or daughter in the last several months.

```
┌──────────────────────────────────────────────────────┐
│            PERSONALITY CHARACTERISTICS                 │
│            OF YOUR 14- TO 16-YEAR-OLD                  │
│                                                        │
│    Type 1              Type 2              Type 3      │
│  ❑ conscientious    ❑ avoids conflict   ❑ blames others│
│  ❑ critical         ❑ impatient         ❑ charming     │
│  ❑ list maker       ❑ independent       ❑ engaging     │
│  ❑ perfectionist    ❑ laid back         ❑ good salesperson│
│  ❑ reliable         ❑ many friends      ❑ lies/manipulates│
│  ❑ scholarly        ❑ mediator          ❑ socially mature│
│  ❑ serious          ❑ rebel             ❑ people person │
│  ❑ well organized   ❑ loyal to peers    ❑ shows off     │
│                                                        │
│  ___ Total          ___ Total           ___Total       │
└──────────────────────────────────────────────────────┘
```

Add up the total in each column. The column with the most checks indicates the pattern characterizing your kids.

Next we need to survey the discipline methods you normally use with your kids, ages fourteen to sixteen. Take a moment and fill out the following chart. Check those methods used, and circle those you feel are successful.

```
┌──────────────────────────────────────────────────────┐
│              DISCIPLINE METHODS USED                   │
│              WITH YOUR 14- TO 16-YEAR-OLD              │
│                                                        │
│   Method              Youth #1        Youth #2         │
│                                                        │
│   1. Bible Study/                                      │
│      Memorization                                      │
│                                                        │
│   2. Bribery                                           │
│                                                        │
│   3. Community                                         │
│      Service                                           │
└──────────────────────────────────────────────────────┘
```

Method	Youth #1	Youth #2
4. Contracting		
5. Cut in Allowance		
6. Family Council		
7. Forced Apologies		
8. Ignoring/ Silent Treatment		
9. Lecturing		
10. Loss of Privileges		
11. More Chores/Work		
12. Parental Strike		
13. Positive Rewards		
14. Put-downs/ Humiliation		
15. Restriction		
16. Spanking/ Hitting		
17. Threatening		
18. Yelling		
19. Other		

List here the three discipline methods you use most often
that are working well—that is, those your kids seem to obey.

	Youth #1	Youth #2
Method One:	_____	_____
Method Two:	_____	_____
Method Three:	_____	_____

What Works, What Doesn't

Now it is time to compare what is working for you with
what worked in the survey families.

DISCIPLINE METHODS RANKED BY "EFFECTIVENESS" AGES 14 TO 16

Discipline Method	Percent Families Where Used	Percent Effective
1. Positive Rewards	55	95
2. Loss of Privileges	62	88
3. Restriction	56	86
4. Family Council	25	80
5. Bible Study/Memorization	14	78
6. Lecturing	77	78
7. More Chores/Work	38	74
8. Contracting	9	67
9. Cut in Allowance	16	66
10. Community Service	10	61
11. Spanking/Hitting	30	61
12. Threatening	41	46
13. Yelling	67	37
14. Bribery	9	37
15. Parental Strike	8	35
16. Forced Apologies	21	35
17. Ignoring	20	33
18. Put-downs/Humiliation	23	19

A reminder as you consider the previous chart: we are just reporting statistics here, not the merits of the methods.

As with the similar table for ages eleven to thirteen, we can learn much from what we see here. It is interesting to note that Positive Rewards remains the most effective method but is used in only about half the families. The least effective method, Put-downs/Humiliation, is still used in nearly a quarter of the homes. Yelling is still used by over two-thirds of the parents, but with poor effectiveness. Spanking or hitting is still used by about a third and it still "works" most of the time—but not nearly as well as earlier. If we want methods that work, we must eliminate Put-downs/Humiliation, Ignoring/Silent Treatment, and Forced Apologies.

If we compare this chart with the one in Chapter 6, we will notice that with the younger teens, thirteen of the eighteen discipline methods worked more than half the time and of these thirteen, eight worked at least 80 percent of the time. But in these middle-teen years things aren't so easy. Eleven of the discipline methods work more than half the time, and only four work 80 percent of the time or better. A lot of stress and frustration is implied in these figures.

Another question on the survey showed this too. The young adults were asked to tell at which age their parents were generally successful with their discipline.

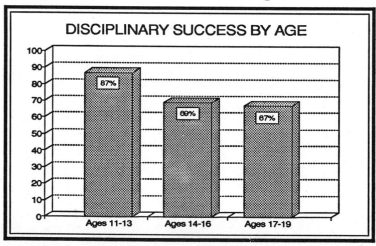

DISCIPLINARY SUCCESS BY AGE

87% — Ages 11-13
69% — Ages 14-16
67% — Ages 17-19

What "type" of young person(s) is living under your roof? Positive Rewards remained the most effective for all three types. Type 1 young people listed the Family Council as the second most effective. This would not be surprising since Type 1 kids tend to be more mentally mature than their siblings or peers. If they were truly first-born they probably received a higher percentage of adult attention in the early years, thus making it more likely for them to respond well to such an adult approach to problem solving. The higher success for Family Council with Type 1 young people was also true in the eleven- to thirteen-year-old category.

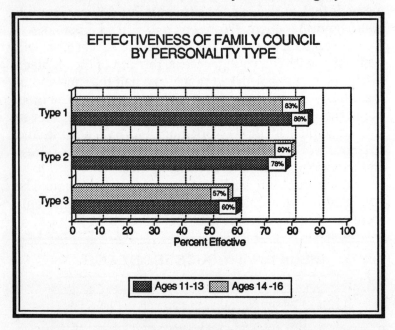

Type 2 teenagers in this age group are not as motivated by money as they were in early adolescence. We saw that cutting allowance worked in nine of ten cases with kids ages eleven to thirteen. But in middle adolescence the success drops to seven in ten.

The survey did not reveal any other major differences in terms of success rates by type of kid this age.

Also, as with the earlier age group, there were no significant differences between guys and girls in the top four
disciplines. Further down the list, however, several methods
were much more effective with girls. Only one method was
much more effective with the guys.

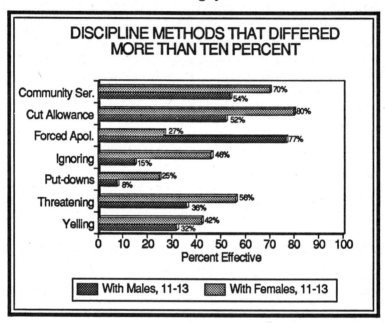

DISCIPLINE METHODS THAT DIFFERED
MORE THAN TEN PERCENT

A look at this graph might suggest that girls are more
sensitive than guys. The negative methods of Ignoring, Put-
downs/Humiliation, Threatening, and Yelling have a much
greater impact on girls. And the effectiveness of Community
Service with girls may have to do with their still being more
mature than the guys.

Why were Forced Apologies dramatically more effective
with guys? Perhaps it is much more humiliating to a guy to
be forced to say something he doesn't want to say. We must
remember, however, that this method is still negative in
nature (maybe even more negative with males because of
the degree of humiliation it produces), and there are probably much better options to use.

Need a Better Option?

If you're considering a change in your disciplinary methods, let's follow the five steps suggested in the previous chapter.

Step 1
Go back a few pages and find the top three discipline methods you are using with your middle adolescent. Write the method in the left-hand column. Search the list for a better, more positive choice. Remember, the better choices are those that can build self-esteem, responsibility, and help the family as a Christian support group.

<u>Most Used Methods</u>   <u>Better Choices</u>

1. _____   _____
2. _____   _____
3. _____   _____

Step 2
Commit your desire to change to the Lord in prayer. Share this with your spouse, close friend, or support group.

Step 3
Apologize to your son or daughter for inappropriate and nonproductive discipline methods you have used in the past. Give them permission to let you know when you slip back into a negative discipline method.

Step 4
With your spouse or close friend, talk through how a better option could have been used in a recent negative discipline situation.

Step 5
Try a better method next time. Easier said than done, right? No one said it would be easy. However, you're halfway there already just by taking the time and trouble to become aware of what needs to be improved and why. As we look at our kids with God's love, we know the stakes are

high, and we feel motivated to make the changes necessary to see improvement in our discipline as necessary.

Some of the young adults who filled out the survey were quick to affirm the fairness and democratic approach their parents took.

- A twenty-year-old female from California said: "Remember that your children are real people with feelings and opinions and need to be treated as though their feelings and opinions are worth listening to."
- A South Carolina, thirty-two-year-old woman advised: "Listen to your children . . . you don't have to agree with them . . . but treat them with respect."
- "No matter how angry you are, no matter how undeserving or stubborn your children are, do not withdraw and refuse to answer their questions," pled a nineteen-year-old Nebraskan. "You will be viewed as a tyrant if you are unapproachable. Firm is okay, cold is an affront."
- "Be fair . . . explain why they are being punished," said a twenty-one-year-old female from Ohio.

Meanwhile, Back in Bed . . .

Phil and Lynn Jones breathe a sigh of relief and a prayer of thanks that David is home, even though it is 1:45 A.M. Within five minutes they are both asleep.

Later that morning Phil, Lynn, and David are at the breakfast table. They're enjoying their Sunday-morning tradition of hot sweet rolls from the local bakery.

David is quiet; he looks tired.

Phil begins: "So, Dave, how'd your night go last night?"

"Oh, good, real good."

"No problems with the car or anything? You know, I just got the carburetor fixed last week," Phil comments.

"It was fine. No problem. I sure appreciate being able to use it. Thanks again."

"What time did you get home last night, Dave?"

"Oh, well, I was a few minutes late. Sorry."

"How late, dear?" his mom asks.

"Oh, around twelve-fifteen, I think. It wasn't bad. We had to finish seeing the movie at Bill's."

Phil looks at Lynn. "Well, son, I guess I don't have to tell you that we're really disappointed. Two things we need to talk about now: you ignored the in-hour we had agreed on last night, and less than one minute ago you lied to us. These hurt, Dave."

Dave says nothing—he's been nailed to the wall, and he knows it.

Lynn looks at her son. "Anything you want to tell us?"

"Well, we finished a movie at midnight and started another one. I really wanted to see it. I'm sorry for being late and for lying. The way I feel now, it wasn't worth it."

Phil reenters the conversation: "We appreciate the apology, and I believe you really are sorry, but you need to conduct yourself more responsibly. What would you say if there was no consequence this time but we established a contract for the future?"

David's eyes brighten. "You mean nothing's going to happen this time? I was afraid you'd ground me."

"Well, that is an option. But let's talk about the future."

"Sure."

"We really believe you can make good choices and want to be responsible. What if we agreed to a contract that will read something like this: 'Phil and Lynn Jones agree to continue to provide David access to the family car on weekends provided (1) specific permission is obtained in advance, (2) a reasonable in-hour is agreed to, and (3) you agree to call home if something comes up that will make you unavoidably late, and (4) you will tell us the truth.'"

Dave replies, "That sounds okay."

Then Phil asks, "Now, what shall we say will be the consequence if you fail to meet these expectations?"

"Well, you've given me plenty of space, that's for sure," Dave says. "Why don't we add that if I blow it again within the next four months I'll lose the use of the car for a month."

Phil nods. "That sounds pretty good. I'll type it up after church and we'll sign while we watch football."

Here we have seen an example of a well-handled discipline situation. The Joneses chose not to confront David when he walked in the door. They knew from previous experience that would result in loud words and high stress for all of them, and it might even wake the neighbors. Better to let David's guilt sink in a little bit. Also they were wise to ask him what time he got in, allowing him the opportunity to be truthful.

Then the discipline method chosen was Contracting, and David even named his own punishment. It might have been a little lighter than Phil and Lynn would have preferred, but they've decided to invest a lot of trust in their son.

Middle adolescence can be a hard time, yet we have looked at ways to teach through discipline in a positive way. Time marches as our young people turn seventeen . . . eighteen . . . nineteen, and we again wonder how to provide loving guidance in the next important stage.

DISCUSSION QUESTIONS

1. Try to remember what you were like as a tenth-grader. What changes had taken place in you from when you were in seventh grade?

2. Briefly describe your own fourteen- to sixteen-year-old physically, mentally, socially, emotionally, and spiritually.

3. How successful were your parents at disciplining you at this age?

4. Compare notes on what chore expectations you have of your fourteen- to sixteen-year-old. Is this going smoothly in your home?

5. Open your Bible to Isaiah 9:6. Which of the four names of Jesus listed mean the most to you as a parent? Why?

8

Ages Seventeen
To Nineteen ⟡

Every stage of adolescent growth has its share of challenges for parents. Later adolescence, however, seems to have more than its share for many families. Think about it: the last two years of high school and the first year out—major league transitions without a doubt! These are years of potential deepening friendship between parents and teenagers. But these are also years when the struggle for independence can become a civil (or not so civil!) war that tears the family apart.

Comparing Notes

Find a group of parents of older teens and we'll find people who are very interested in comparing notes and ideas. Let's listen in on three couples as they sit around the coffee table late one night.

Mr. Green: Sometimes I'm so frustrated with my eighteen-year-old son. He doesn't seem to pay any attention to us anymore.

Mrs. Green: And we're both so tired when we come home from work, it's just easier not to pay much attention to what he's up to most of the time.

116

Mrs. Simpson: I know what you mean. But I have to keep reminding myself that parenting is one job I can't quit.

Mr. Simpson: I feel that the only influence I have with our two teenagers is when I come to them as their friend and talk things out. When I'm heavy-handed, they tune me out; I can see it all over their faces! Most of the time I succeed at being a friend—but it sure takes extra effort to remember to take the time to enter their lives.

Mrs. Sills: How do you enter their lives? I sure couldn't call our kids my friends.

Mr. Sills: She's right about that; I feel the same way.

Mr. Simpson: Unfortunately, I'm rarely home for dinner because I get home from work so late and the kids need to eat early so they can get to the game, play rehearsal, youth group, or whatever. So I try to knock on their bedroom door around ten-thirty a couple of nights a week. I just sit on the floor next to the bed and see how the day has gone. It's not much, but it helps.

Mr. Sills: You make it sound so easy. I find myself yelling a lot when I want them to do something.

Mrs. Sills: And if they resist, I give them a sweet little speech about how much I love them and on and on . . . I guess I'm laying a guilt trip on them. It works sometimes, but I wouldn't call us a family with a lot of unity.

Mrs. Simpson: If we haven't established a good relationship with our kids by the time they hit late high school, we really won't have much influence anymore.

Mr. Green: I'm afraid you're right, but I wish it weren't so. It would be so much easier if I could just say the word and they'd obey without question.

Mr. Simpson: Our kids do pretty well at obeying us when we really talk things out—and they understand why we've said what we've said. Like last month, Jill, our seventeen-year-old, wanted the car and . . .

We'll come back to this conversation later. It's not hard to see that two of these couples are really struggling to figure out how to make things work in their families. They see the approach taken by the Simpsons and envy what they see, but that approach in their own families is a long way away.

As we have done with the other age groups, let's try to remind ourselves what is normal.

Normal Patterns

Physically

For just about everyone, all the pieces have finally come together. The vast majority will have reached their adult height by the end of this stage. Most will have huge stores of energy that will be reflected in hectic schedules, multiple interests, and late nights. Awareness of one's own body is not as intense as in the earlier years. While there is still much mental comparing, a lot of comfort is derived in that everyone looks about the same.

Mentally

While girls may still tend to think more deeply than a lot of the guys, most guys are no dummies either. They can think, reason, and ponder. What is it that they are pondering? More so than when they were age fourteen to sixteen, many are giving serious consideration to their future careers. The decision whether or not to attend college, and if so, which one, looms large in the minds of most seniors. They can see implications for choice A compared to choice B or C.

• *Implications for discipline:* As with middle adolescents, coercive disciplines like Yelling, Threatening, and Put-downs/ Humiliation are despised. This age group wants to be treated like young adults. They want their opinions listened to and considered by their parents; they want their ability to make decisions to be respected.

Socially

Some of the tight bonding and grouping so characteristic of the earlier stages begins to unravel during this period.

Some young people become individualistic and owe their loyalties to no specific group at the school, but are cordial with all and contentedly so. The end of the senior year marks a time of sentimental reflection on the friendships and associations over the years. After graduation many will never see one another again.

Group dating and single dating become commonplace as guys and girls try to figure out what they like and what they don't like in someone of the opposite sex. Some of the girls are definitely thinking about weddings, marriage, and babies.

• *Implications for discipline:* In these years kids need room—room to explore the options open to them in developing various relationships and interests. This isn't easy for us parents because it means we need to begin to let go and allow our kids to make some mistakes.

Many parents shift their approach at this age. Instead of laying down the law on every issue that comes up or even offering their advice or opinions, they sit back and are happily available when needed. One twenty-three-year-old female from Georgia who took the survey gives some advice to parents:

> As your [teenagers] grow, you need to grow with them and loosen your grip! When it is time to let go, *let go!* If and when they need parental support and advice, as the outsider, help them see the pros and cons of the situation and also, hopefully, you as a parent will be strong enough in God so you can relate to them the Scriptures.

The respect our kids have for us will come more from our relationship with them than from our position of authority. We'll talk more about letting go in Chapter 9.

Emotionally

Even more than in the previous stage, this age young person has the capacity to empathize and feel deeply about an issue or a person. This is both a blessing and a curse. If things are going well for him or her with the opposite sex, for example, the young person will be very happy. Unfortunately, if this is a problem area, the depth of his or her sadness will be deep indeed.

• *Implications for discipline:* It is the experience of many parents that their sons and daughters in this age group do not come to them for emotional support or advice. By age twenty, they will have become completely independent from the family. Efforts by the parent to hang on will make the nineteen-year-old feel he or she is being treated like a child. If your late adolescent confides in you, treat it as a gift. If not, respect his or her need to finish the task of separating emotionally from you.

Spiritually

Spiritual development parallels mental development in many respects. In this stage the young person usually completes much of his or her decision making about the issues of faith and lifestyle. Those who have decided to take a stand for Christ may do so with astonishing boldness. Those who have decided to forget the whole thing will do so in this period. They are making up their own minds—and one method of expressing independence from the parent is to reject the parent's belief system. Still others may come out of a highly structured church youth program in high school and begin to drift spiritually in college. In this new chapter of their lives, it may take them awhile to become responsible for their own spiritual growth.

• *Implications for discipline:* The subject of what kind of parenting style is most effective in passing along moral belief and faith has received some academic attention over the years. One study asked two hundred college students to reflect on the style their parents used while they were adolescents, and compare their own beliefs now with those of their parents. The results revealed that the worst parental approach—most ineffective in transferring religious beliefs—is ignoring/permissive combined with low nurturance.[1] (In

Chapter 3 you determined your own parenting style and level of nurturance.)

The same study found that high nurturance and high control in the earlier years is most instrumental in passing on beliefs. Also, while a very nurturing mom impacted the beliefs of daughters in a positive way, the father's nurturance heavily influenced *both* sons and daughters.[2]

There is hope for the Christian family to be a real support group during these years. Whether or not this actually happens depends partly on the spiritual depth of the teenager. Just as important, however, is the willingness of the parent to admit weakness, need for growth, and to help the teenager feel that he or she is not being treated like a child spiritually.

Normal Issues

Mr. Green: I'll tell you what we struggle with in our family. It's the car. They're both drivers now, and they think they should both be able to drive off without even asking or telling us where they are going and when they'll be back.

Mrs. Sills: Our son has already had two tickets and one accident—and he's only been driving since just before his seventeenth birthday!

Mr. Simpson: I've compared notes with a lot of other parents and it looks to me that we can expect *at least* two tickets and an accident from each of our kids before they turn twenty. Many kids are much worse than that.

Mr. Sills: I'm not so concerned about a couple of tickets and a fender bender. It's our daughter's grades. She's involved in so many things she's not doing as well as she needs to do to get into a good college.

Mrs. Green: Our son is struggling with what he wants to do with his life. He's in his first year at the university and still has no clue about his future.

Mrs. Simpson: That is hard for us too. Our first-born wants to be a teacher. She's had that figured out for years. Our second-born son, though . . . he's just into having a good time. Don't bother *him* with the future.

Does any of this sound familiar? Issues of concern have shifted from personal habits (ages eleven to thirteen) and household responsibilities and rules (fourteen to sixteen) to outside issues: the car, the school, and the future.

Normal Parenting

How do Christian parents approach their older teenagers? In the families represented in the survey, another big shift takes place compared with the earlier stages.

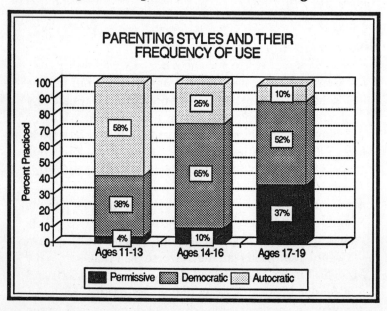

Compared with the previous stage, an autocratic style drops by more than half, a democratic style dips a little, and a permissive style is up nearly quadruple.

But how did these college-age people perceive the success of their parents' discipline during this period? The following graph illustrates.

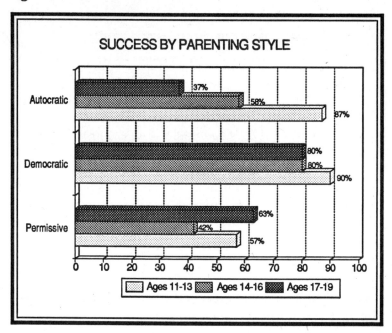

Compared to the previous stage, the democratic/equalitarian styles are still the most successful and at exactly the same percentage. Autocratic/authoritarian is 20 percent less successful and permissive/ignoring is 20 percent more successful than reported for ages fourteen to sixteen. Based on what we've learned about adolescent stages, there's not much surprise in this, is there?

Your Late Adolescent and the Disciplines You Use

Take a moment and consider your late adolescent. On the following page, check the characteristics you have seen as generally true about your son or daughter in the last several months.

Then add up the total checks in each column. The column with the most checks will indicate a pattern of behavior that characterizes your older teen. If you have younger teens, go back and compare types.

PERSONALITY CHARACTERISTICS
OF YOUR 17- TO 19-YEAR-OLD

Type 1	Type 2	Type 3
❏ conscientious	❏ avoids conflict	❏ blames others
❏ critical	❏ impatient	❏ charming
❏ list maker	❏ independent	❏ engaging
❏ perfectionist	❏ laid back	❏ good salesperson
❏ reliable	❏ many friends	❏ lies/manipulates
❏ scholarly	❏ mediator	❏ socially mature
❏ serious	❏ rebel	❏ people person
❏ well organized	❏ loyal to peers	❏ shows off
___ Total	___ Total	___Total

As in Chapters 6 and 7, we need to survey the discipline methods you normally use with this age son or daughter. Take a moment and fill out the following chart.

DISCIPLINE METHODS USED
WITH YOUR 17- TO 19-YEAR-OLD

Method	Youth #1	Youth #2
1. Bible Study/ Memorization		
2. Bribery		
3. Community Service		
4. Contracting		
5. Cut in Allowance		
6. Family Council		

Method	Youth #1	Youth #2
7. Forced Apologies		
8. Ignoring/ Silent Treatment		
9. Lecturing		
10. Loss of Privileges		
11. More Chores/Work		
12. Parental Strike		
13. Positive Rewards		
14. Put-downs/ Humiliation		
15. Restriction		
16. Spanking/ Hitting		
17. Threatening		
18. Yelling		
19. Other		

List here the three discipline methods you use most often and feel are working well—that is, that your kids obey.

	Youth #1	Youth #2
Method One:	_____	_____
Method Two:	_____	_____
Method Three:	_____	_____

What Works, What Doesn't

We might wonder sometimes if *anything* works with this age group. In nearly four hundred families represented in the survey, we can see that some discipline methods were still successful much of the time.

DISCIPLINE METHODS RANKED BY "EFFECTIVENESS" AGES 17 TO 19		
Discipline Method	Percent Families Where Used	Percent Effective
1. Positive Rewards	48	92
2. Loss of Privileges	48	85
3. Parental Strike	9	80
4. Lecture	68	79
5. Contracting	28	76
6. Bible Study/Memorization	11	76
7. More Chores/Work	26	75
8. Restriction	41	73
9. Community Service	11	64
10. Family Council	44	52
11. Cut in Allowance	11	48
12. Ignoring	9	45
13. Spanking	16	37
14. Threatening	35	34
15. Put-downs/Humiliation	21	28
16. Bribery	8	25
17. Yelling	51	25
18. Forced Apologies were not used in any of the families surveyed for this age group.		

Just as there was a big difference in effective discipline methods between early adolescence and middle adolescence, there is a rather large difference as we progress from middle adolescence to this stage. Positive Rewards and Loss of Privileges remain the most effective discipline methods.

Remember that Positive Rewards constitute more of a discipline *preventative* measure. When we affirm, acknowledge, and reward the good we see in our teenagers, we motivate them toward more good.

That discipline becomes a much more difficult task at this age can be seen in the preceding list, where only three methods have an 80 percent or better success rate. There were eight methods that had this success rate for the younger teens, and four when we looked at the middle teens.

There is much less similarity among Christian families in this age group too. Only two methods were used by more than 50 percent of the families represented in the survey: Lecturing and Yelling! Of these two methods, only Lecturing has some potential to build self-esteem, build responsibility, and perhaps build the family as a Christian community. It is a sad fact that Yelling is used in 51 percent of the families, yet it was tied at the bottom of the list as the *least successful* discipline method.

It is interesting to see the Parental Strike move into third place in this age; it was fifteenth place in both the other age groups. It may be that late adolescents are more capable than younger teenagers of connecting the inconvenience and implication of the Parental Strike to their own irresponsibility.

The Parental Strike, properly done, is a wonderful attention-getter and certainly motivates the young person to think seriously about the behavior in question!

The survey revealed that the different discipline methods worked similarly among all types of young people in this age category. There were two exceptions, however. Type 2 teenagers were found to be much more responsive to restriction and More Chores/Work than their Type 1 and Type 3 counterparts.

Male/female differences were not significant in the top three most successful disciplines. However, as you can see from the graph on the following page, there were some differences lower on the list that may need to be taken into consideration when choosing an appropriate method for sons and daughters.

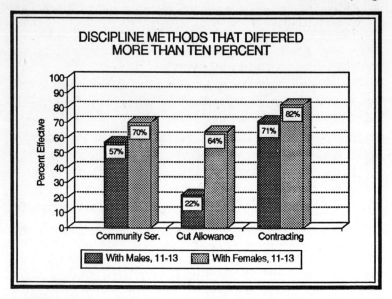

DISCIPLINE METHODS THAT DIFFERED
MORE THAN TEN PERCENT

We can also see that the girls are more responsive than the guys in these three methods at this particular age.

Need a Better Option?

If you have a seventeen- to nineteen-year-old, the five steps that have been outlined for the younger ages can also be applied here.

Step 1

Go back a few pages, find your top three discipline methods for this age group, and write them in the left-hand column below. In the right-hand column write a better, more positive choice if necessary. Remember, the better choice is always one that builds self-esteem, builds responsibility, or helps the family to be a Christian support group.

	Most Used Methods	Better Choices
1.	_____	_____
2.	_____	_____
3.	_____	_____

Step 2

Commit your desire to change to the Lord in prayer. Share this with your spouse, a close friend, and/or support group.

Step 3

Apologize to your son or daughter for inappropriate and nonproductive discipline methods you have used in the past. Let them know they have the right to gently call it to your attention if you regress to a negative method.

Step 4

With your spouse or close friend, talk through how a better discipline method could have been used in a recent negative situation.

Step 5

Try a better method next time.

With this age young person it's helpful to know some of the different approaches to conflict resolution. One popular approach is "Parent Effectiveness Training."[3] Though PET is not specifically a Christian approach, one of the helpful key principles is distinguishing between "I messages" and "you messages." (We'll hear this explained in a practical example when we listen in again on our three couples.) Another key principle of PET is using a "no lose" method of resolving a situation that has become a conflict.

Here are the suggested steps[4] (do these *together* with your son or daughter):

1. Identify and define the conflict/problem.
2. Generate alternative possible solutions.
3. Evaluate alternate solutions.
4. Decide mutually on the best solution.
5. Determine ways to implement the agreed-on solution.
6. Later, evaluate how it's going.

This is called a "no lose" method because both parent and young person make major contributions to the process and agree on the solution after examining alternatives. The rea-

son this method works with late adolescents is that it vali-
dates appropriate independence while encouraging a high
degree of communication and mutual decision making with
parents. Also, by this stage they are able to think through
different alternative solutions and visualize their potential
outcomes. (This is not a good method, however, to use with
twelve-year-old boys, about whom it could be said, "The
lights are on but no one is home.")

The Simpsons have used this method with their seventeen-year-old daughter. They have practiced this approach
and it comes pretty easy for them now. Let's go back to our
living room eavesdropping. Mr. Simpson is about to share a
recent situation they faced.

Back Around the Coffee Table

Mr. Simpson: Our kids do pretty well when it comes to
obeying us—*if* we really talk things out and they understand
why we say what we say. For example, a little over a
month ago Jill, our seventeen-year-old, wanted the car. It
was something like the seventh or eighth night in a row
we'd let her take it for one of her many activities and I was
getting a little frustrated.

I said, "Jill, you're a responsible young lady and you
know how much I appreciate you. I feel frustrated, though,
that you are out so many nights in a row with the car. It's
not that I don't trust you, I just wonder if you really need
to use the car so often."

Mrs. Simpson: We've learned to use "I messages" instead of
"you messages" when dealing with teenagers. Notice that
he said, "I feel frustrated . . ." instead of "You are exploit-
ing our generosity as parents." "You messages" tend to be
triggers for conflict and it's easy to combine a "you
message" with a put-down like, "You're late again; you're
so irresponsible." Especially with Jill, who is our second-
born, "you messages" immediately send defenses up.

Mr. Sills: I have a sinking feeling in my stomach.

Mrs. Simpson: Why?

Mr. Sills: I'm always saying "You this" or "You that" with my teenagers. You're sure right about it sending their defenses sky high.

Mr. Simpson: It took us several months to break the "you message" habit. Susan and I both agreed to let each other know if we heard the other one talking that way. We asked the kids to keep us accountable too. They were shocked that we came to them for this kind of help, but they really appreciated it. I think it raised the value of our parental respect stock several points.

Mrs. Green: So what happened with Jill?

Mr. Simpson: Jill explained that she had made arrangements to meet a friend at the mall to do some shopping. I told her okay, but that I wanted us to both think about the issue and talk about it when she returned.

Mrs. Simpson: Ted and I talked it over while Jill was gone. We both would like her home more, but we had to admit that she was already getting excellent grades in school and that the activities she was going to were fine. She's almost eighteen and we have basically given over the responsibility to make her own decisions about use of time.

Mr. Simpson: So, we agreed that we'd ignore that issue but at least get her to agree to help with paying for gas. Things have been tight for us financially, and we thought it could help teach her to be more responsible if she connected the freedom of driving to the cost of driving.

Mrs. Simpson: When she came home we had a fire going in the fireplace and had a real good talk. She thought we were going to come at her with some sort of "must be home X number of nights" approach, and she was surprised when we said that was one option, but unless she was in favor of it, we didn't want to go in that direction.

Mr. Sills: I bet she dropped that one fast!

Mr. Simpson: You're right! We talked about the money problems we'd been having and the possibility of her paying more than 50 percent of her part of the insurance as she does now, plus helping with gas. We went over the pros and cons of both and settled on her paying for use of the car on a ten-cents-per-mile basis.

Mrs. Simpson: She was surprised to hear that when you use your car in your job, you have to keep track of mileage, so it wasn't that uncommon. She's got a little notebook that she keeps in the glove compartment and has been real good about keeping track.

Mr. Simpson: I've double-checked her figures twice with the odometer and she's been right on each time. She pays up once a week, on Saturday.

Mr. Green: By the way you're smiling, I can almost predict what you're going to say next.

Mr. Simpson: You got it. In the four weeks since starting this, she's been out with the car only three nights each week. A friend has picked her up a few times, but otherwise she's been at home.

Mrs. Green: Looks as if you taught her to be responsible, got her to stay home more, and got some help with money—all without a threat or a raised voice.

Mrs. Simpson: It doesn't always turn out so well. We've had failure, too, but this one worked well.

Here we have seen some wise handling of a problem situation using a rather informal application of the no-lose conflict resolution method suggested in Parent Effectiveness Training. It basically involved a mini Family Council where the parties involved worked out the problem. If Jill was the kind of girl who needed more structure, a formal contract may have been in order along with a negotiated "number of nights at home" agreement. Additionally, the Simpsons figured that use of the car was a positive enough reward and that they would continue to commend the good decisions their daughter was already making.

In this section we have looked in some detail at the application of discipline methods at different ages. As we consider making improvement in disciplining our teen-agers, what additional positive steps are there to keep in mind?

DISCUSSION QUESTIONS

1. If you and your parents had conflicts when you were ages seventeen to nineteen, what were the issues?

2. How is it going with you and your late adolescent? What issues create conflict for you?

3. At this age, where were you spiritually compared with your parents? How does your own seventeen- to nineteen-year-old compare with you spiritually now?

4. The author states that the success of "belief transference" rests largely on the nurturing behavior of the parents toward the teenager. How are you doing at showing support and love toward your teenager?

5. Open your Bible to Ephesians 1:16–19. Paul's prayer is a wonderful way for a parent to pray for a son or daughter. What are the main ideas in the prayer? Which do you feel most urgently needs to be answered right now in the life of your son or daughter?

SECTION III

MAKING
POSITIVE CHANGES

9

An Ounce of Prevention

We've taken a look at our teenagers—what they're like and what methods of discipline and guidance might work with them at each age level. We've tried to understand ourselves and what our style of parenting is; also what perspective Scripture gives us on the whole issue. But now (drumroll, trumpet fanfare, royal fireworks display!) it's time to turn our attention to positive changes.

There is so much we can do, in God's strength, to change things for the better. As we said in the opening pages, this is a book of *hope* and *help*. Sometimes we parents feel that both are in short supply. We get discouraged because we experience failure and frustration. Yet because we are parents who care about our kids, are motivated to see improvement, and have the power of God living within, there is hope!

It's not too late to start—or too early! There is much you can do right now as a parent to reduce the need for discipline. If you have a five- or six-year-old, how you relate to your child now can make a profound difference when that child hits puberty. On the other hand, if you've got a seventeen-year-old living under your roof, you've still got time to make positive changes. Let's dive in!

Remembering What Is Normal

Much of what was said in Chapters 5–8 was to help us realize what is normal for teenagers. Let's see if we really grasp the difference this can make in our discipline.

> *Case One:* Your thirteen-year-old daughter is a real klutz and seems to have a habit of tripping and knocking into things. Today she knocked over a lamp, which fell against a wall, which knocked a picture down. The glass in the frame shattered. Your response is . . .
>
> *Case Two:* You pass your twelve-year-old son's room and hear rock music being played on his radio. You . . .
>
> *Case Three:* You used to have good communication with your son, but now, at age sixteen, he has become very uncommunicative. About all he does is grunt. In this situation you . . .
>
> *Case Four:* You happen to go into your seventeen-year-old daughter's room to put something away, and notice two issues of *Bride's* magazine. She has a fairly steady boyfriend. Your response is . . .

Being aware of what is normal for the age of our teenager may remove some of the compulsion to discipline or panic in the cases stated above. What insight does "normality" give us in these situations?

Case One: A normal thirteen-year-old's body is growing and changing rapidly. Clumsiness is absolutely normal. Punishment would be wrong in this situation. Any discipline beyond asking her to help clean up the mess and perhaps chip in to replace the broken glass would be inappropriate as well.

Case Two: Remember that your early adolescent is beginning to need to stake out a separate identity from you as a parent. The easiest avenues of independence for him at this age are: music, choice of friends, how his room looks, and clothes. Coming down hard on the boy in this situation will probably increase his resolve to listen to secular rock all the more. Use it as a door to open communication instead of closing it. Ask what he likes about it. Listen to a song or two and talk about what the words are saying. Ask him if the words are in agreement with what he knows God wants.

Case Three: A sixteen-year-old boy has a lot on his mind, literally. Whole new vistas are opening to him as his mind is now able to "think about a thought." Also, he is expressing his independence by controlling the information flow. Don't try to pry information out of him; it will only make it worse. Be patient. Most "grunters" begin talking again eventually.

Case Four: Don't panic. Your seventeen-year-old daughter has apparently already answered the questions of early adolescence (who am I?) and middle adolescence (where am I going?). Now she's mentally working on the question of late adolescence, "Who's going with me?" Her thoughts about weddings, honeymoons, and babies probably have little connection to her current boyfriend. Don't put her down or try to talk her out of these very normal interests. Use them instead as triggers for heart-to-heart communication. Ask what she has begun to see are important things to look for in a husband. Let her express her feelings about what she sees as important to make a marriage work. What difference does she see that God can make?

Have you ever noticed how parents treat third- and fourth-born children compared to those that are first- and second-born? Normally, parents are much easier on the later two—they now know what kids are like. They've not only learned it from their own kids but also by observing the children of their friends. Knowing what is normal at different stages affects the way they respond.

Developing Family Support

Looking at the family as a spiritual support group for its members may reduce the need for discipline or correction. Don't dismiss the idea that a family really can be a team in Christ. Many families are—but it doesn't happen that way by accident.

When our kids were small they looked at us with more or
less awe. We had their respect because of our position of
authority. In contrast, we won't find too many teenagers
who look at their parents with awe because of anything—
especially not the position of authority their parents are
supposed to have. Instead, we will have their respect only
because of the *relationship* we have with them. In fact, without a good relationship we will not have much of anything
with our teenagers.

What are the essentials of a good relationship—a family
team spirit—and how do these essentials reduce the need for
discipline?

The Communication Factor

We saw in Chapter 3 how important it is to explain our
expectations and discipline to a young person. If our kid is
angry and wants to argue, however, it probably isn't the best
time to talk things out. In that case, we might want to say, "I
will not discuss this with you right now; all you want to do
is argue. We'll talk later." This is better than "Because I said
so!" because it gives a reason you are choosing to cut the
conversation short.

Even if the circumstances are not strained, "Because I said
so" will not be adequate for a fourteen-year-old. Many
parents constantly slam the door of communication on their
teenager and later wonder why their son or daughter won't
open up anymore.

How do you react when your son or daughter shares a
hurt or a need?

a. Quick advice (worth about a nickel).[1]

Daughter: Mom, things went badly today at school. Jana has
   started to be better friends with Mary and was really cold
   to me.
Mom: Well, you have lots of other friends at school. I never
   liked Jana much anyway. You're better off without her.

Is this daughter going to feel like talking anymore? Not likely. Her mom has slammed the door of communication in her face. Quick advice is one of the most common adult responses to a teen who reveals a need, and it kills communication.

b. Reassurance (treating your kid like a puppy dog).

Daughter: Mom, things went badly at school today. Jana has started to be better friends with Mary and was really cold to me.

Mom: That's too bad, dear. Cheer up, I'm sure things will work out. They always do, you know. Pray about it, okay? I'm sure God has a reason for what happened.

How likely is the daughter to feel like talking more this time? Not very. Has her mom listened to her hurt? Hardly. Has her syrupy song been of any real help in the situation? Not really.

c. Identifying (probing for more as the door opens).

Daughter: Mom, things went badly at school today. Jana has started to be better friends with Mary and was really cold to me.

Mom: I'm sorry, hon. What happened?

Daughter: A bunch of things. She sat with Mary at lunch and left me by myself.

Mom: What else?

Daughter: I heard that she told Samantha she thought I dressed funny.

Mom: How did that make you feel?

Daughter: I was mad, then really hurt.

Mom: How did you feel about what happened at lunch?

Daughter: I felt like I was getting dumped. I felt worthless. And I feel like I'm going to have no one to be with now.

Mom: Did this just start today? I mean, all of a sudden?

Daughter: (explains)

In this response the parent begins by asking questions, probing not only for information but for feelings as well. It opens the door wider and wider. The young person feels listened to and respected.

d. Self-revealing (life wasn't perfect for you either).

Daughter: Mom, things went badly at school today. Jana has started being better friends with Mary and was really cold to me.

Mom: Wow, that sure sounds familiar.

Daughter: What do you mean?

Mom: That happened to me so many times when I was growing up, I thought I had a disease that made me poisonous or something. It really hurts, doesn't it?

Is this conversation over? No, it's just begun, well on its way to being deep and meaningful for both mother and daughter. The mother has thrown the door wide open. (Of course, self-revealing is inappropriate if we don't have a similar experience to share. We shouldn't make something up! Also, we mustn't get so involved in *our* story that we forget who we're supposed to be listening to.)

Probably the best progression in communicating with our teen when a need or hurt is shared is to begin with *identifying*, then move to *self-revealing* if we can, and then our *advice* and *reassurance* will be appropriate and respected.

In a home where this pattern of communication is commonplace, it's not hard to see that something very good is happening. Kids are talking; parents are listening, relating compassionately, and offering advice sparingly. When there is need for discipline it is given and received in the context of a positive relationship.

This relationship base is crucial to whatever success we hope to have as parents when it comes to discipline and correction. A positive relationship between parents and teens will reduce the need for discipline because our sons and daughters will *want* to please us. They will resist doing wrong because they know it will hurt us and hurt their relationship with us.

The Friendship Factor

It is possible to be friends with our kids. This is another component of having our family feel like a Christian support group. Sure, we are the parents, and they are the kids—no one is going to deny that. Yet, in our day-to-day relationships with them our attitude can include more mutual growth, learning, and enjoyment as opposed to our always taking the authority role.

Are we open with our kids about our own failures and struggles? Do we ask them for their advice and opinion from time to time? Do we ask them to pray for us about the stresses we face? Can they see that we enjoy them—that we not only love them but like them too?

When teenagers size up potential friends, most will look for qualities that include a good sense of humor, someone who enjoys life and can have fun, but also someone who is genuine, caring, understanding, and dependable. If you were a teenager, and *your* parents had the same qualities you exhibit right now, would *you* want a friendship with them?

One thing you can count on about young people and their friends: they will go to almost any length not to hurt them. Parents who succeed in being friends with their kids will reduce the amount of discipline necessary.

If our kids are growing Christians we have another big plus. They know they are to obey us as parents (Ephesians 6:1). In a family where parents and kids are friends, the parents are trying, in God's strength, to obey Ephesians 6:4 (to not provoke their children). As kids see us model real Christianity in the home, we are much more likely to receive their respect and cooperation.

The Praise Factor

We have already seen in Chapter 4 that using Positive Rewards is a good preventative discipline method. When

we get better at affirming the good we see in our kids, we
motivate them to make good choices.

Jim's dad stops by his son's room on his way to the den.
"Say, Jim, nice job on the lawn. It looks great and I really
appreciate how you put everything away. That really helps.
Thanks a lot."

That praise didn't take even one minute, but little affirma-
tions like it—if done sincerely—will communicate a positive
spirit within the home. The son or daughter will feel the
respect and appreciation of the parents. Most kids prefer
praise to criticism or nagging. Our praise can help shape
their behavior positively, reducing the need for discipline.

Like Money in the Bank

When good communication, friendship, and affirmation
are demonstrated in the home, it is like making deposits of
goodwill into the bank of family unity. Times will come,
even in the best families, when kids will make poor choices.
These poor choices will need to be dealt with, and as we
administer discipline or correction, we are making a withdrawal on what we have deposited in the past. Our kids are
likely to receive our discipline and modify their behavior
partly because they want to please the Lord, but also because
they don't want to disrupt the good thing they have going
in their family.

Many of the teenagers who filled out the discipline survey
were quite free in sharing why they choose to obey their
parents. Many of the answers reflected the importance of
relationship and love.

- "When I had done something *really* wrong, my parents
  were supportive, understanding, and loving. I was able to
  see that they cared" (nineteen-year-old male, Georgia).
- "When I saw their love and concern, it overcame my urge
  to disobey" (twenty-two-year-old male, Minnesota).
- "Their love for me, their friendship with me, their sacrific-
  ing for me, their being honest and transparent with me"
  (twenty-year-old female, Minnesota).

- "I attribute my parents' success in discipline of me during my adolescent years to their commitment to the Lord Jesus Christ and their modeling of a godly life" (twenty-one-year-old female, Georgia).

Building Self-Esteem

Books abound on the importance of building self-esteem in children and teenagers. It doesn't take a Ph.D. in social psychology to understand that kids who feel good about themselves will be far less likely to succumb to negative peer pressure. A young person who is not inclined to do wrong things will be in less need of correction. There are specific things we can do as parents to help our sons and daughters in this area. And the earlier we begin, the better.

One family took this idea very seriously. Wanting their kids to enter adolescence with at least one skill the teenager could feel good about, the parents made some intentional decisions when each of their kids turned five. Each of them would have a specialty.

With their first five-year-old, they encouraged the specialty of photography. By age eight she had her business license from the state and her own pet-and-people photography business. Two or three nights a month she and her father spent time together on this specialty, which has turned into quite a profitable enterprise. As this daughter entered middle school she did so with a positive self-image. Not surprisingly, she was the only one in a school of a thousand junior highers to have this skill and her own business.

With their second five-year-old, these parents encouraged the specialty of keyboard performance. She began keyboard lessons at that age and by late elementary school was playing not only in school and at nursing homes but also enjoyed playing short programs for weary shoppers in the larger department stores and malls.

The third five-year-old was encouraged in the specialty of making people happy. She soon had her own clown outfit, complete with a huge rainbow wig, and worked with her father two or three nights a month on learning clowning and developing a program of tricks. She takes that program to church families, both old and young, to the delight of all.

We may not have the luxury of a seven-year lead time to build the self-esteem of our teenagers. We can, however, help them see what their strengths are and build on those strengths. We can help them get involved in activities that are positive and upbuilding.

Sure, even a good and godly teenager with excellent self-esteem is going to make bad choices from time to time. Loving correction will need to take place. Yet it's easy to see that that young person is going to need disciplining far fewer times than the young person who is insecure, feeling inferior, and a sitting duck for negative peer influence.

Giving Responsibility and Respect

A nineteen-year-old female from Minnesota wrote:

> I feel the reason I obeyed [my parents] is because the older I became the more responsibility they gave me. I was able to express my opinion when I was younger, and even if they did not agree with me, they would explain to me their reasons . . . I have a high respect for my parents, and now they leave the decisions up to me, but they do give me their opinions still. I do take what they say very seriously.

Would you guess this girl was in constant need of discipline from her parents? Hardly. She felt real responsibility had been given to her as she was growing up. It showed that her parents trusted her and she respected them for it.

What kinds of responsibilities do parents give their kids as they mature? Many parents link successful handling of household chores with increased freedom. Some of the following might be appropriate with your own young person.

FREEDOMS EARNED
THROUGH RESPONSIBILITY

<u>Responsibilities</u>   <u>Freedoms</u>

Early Adolescence

Do own laundry, occasional meal preparation, yard work, limited car maintenance. Use of money, decide when to go to bed, menu selection, clothing allowance.

Middle Adolescence

Regular menu and meal preparation, pay for own clothes, learn about family budget system, more car maintenance. Use of family car, generous weekend "in" hours, part-time job.

Late Adolescence

Home remodeling projects, major car maintenance, help with family finances (car insurance, etc.) Own car, curfew dropped, "inform" parents of whereabouts rather than ask permission,* out-of-town trips.

(*Parents do have the right—and responsibility—to set broad moral limits for anyone living under their roof, but older teens should not have to get permission for otherwise acceptable activities.)

As parents we now have a feel for which of these may appeal to our own teenagers. Whatever we choose, we show our respect as we give them genuine responsibility coupled with genuine freedoms. A young person who is learning responsibility and being rewarded for it will see the benefits of cooperation. He or she would have too much to lose through rebellion.

Helping Teens Spiritually

As a young person grows in his or her relationship with
Christ, the fruit of the Spirit and the characteristics of love
will be more and more evident in the life lived at home. We
can't slip "spirituality pills" into the breakfast cereal (though
it's an appealing thought). So how do we help our kids grow
spiritually?

1. We model a growing Christian life ourselves.

Spirituality is much better caught than taught. Are we
seeing answers to prayer? Are we are experiencing His
power? Are we are seeing things in our lives and that of our
family that can be explained only by the presence and power
of God? If so, we are well on our way to profoundly influencing our young people spiritually.

2. We allow ourselves to be vulnerable.

Say what? Our kids need to see us acknowledge that we
are not perfect, that we have problems, too, and that we are
trusting the power of Christ to work change in our lives. Yes,
we probably have more Bible knowledge than our sons and
daughters, but teenagers and parents alike face the daily
challenge of living the Christian life.

It's easy to always put ourselves in the teacher role. After
all, we're the parents, right? The problem with this approach
is that our kids will see our imperfections, even if we won't
admit them. And what will they call the gap between our
talk and our walk? They'll call it hypocrisy, and it will drive
them away from a relationship with the Savior.

3. We reveal genuine joy in our lives.

Kids are attracted to life. Ask teenagers who their favorite
teacher is at school and chances are, they'll describe someone who has a real zest for life. Our deep relationship with
Jesus Christ as parents should result in a joy that our kids
will see. No, we don't have to be a "life of the party" kind of
person, but we do need to evidence joy of life.

Letting Go

Most parents do not envision their son or daughter still living at home at age twenty-five, as dependent on Mom and Dad as if the "kid" were thirteen. We intuitively realize that we've got to eventually let loose—but it's hard.

Seeing our kids grow older reminds us that we're aging too. We may feel guilty for "not doing a good enough job" raising our kids so we want to keep control as long as possible to accomplish last-minute adjustments. We may feel powerless in other areas of our lives, but at home we feel we still have power and we're going to use it as long as possible. Or we may have trouble letting go because our whole lives are wrapped up in our kids.

One or more of these reasons may convince us to keep hanging on, but we're not doing our kids a favor. Refusing to let go also greatly increases the likelihood of rebellion. Remember in our survey, we learned that only 37 percent of seventeen- to nineteen-year-olds report being obedient to their parents who were autocratic or authoritarian. Not letting go is a classic symptom of this approach to parenting. It might work with eleven-year-olds, but it doesn't work when they're nineteen.

Ray and Anne Ortlund make a good suggestion about letting go of our kids: tell them in advance that it *is* going to happen.

> We know that from now on, the Lord will be coming more and more into your life, and the more we see you getting your orders from Him, the more we can back off. Probably by the time you're twenty we won't have to tell you what to do at all. You'll be getting your orders from God, and we'll just be your good friends.[2]

This approach conveys trust, respect, and confidence. Of course it means painfully having to watch our kids make some mistakes. It will mean helping them mop up some of the messes they create. But most kids will learn responsibility and gain some wisdom in the process.

Many of the survey respondents commented on the importance of letting go. When asked what advice they would give to parents about discipline, an eighteen-year-old male and twenty-year-old female said this:

- "Don't be so picky and strict. Let the child live a little and get into a little trouble. Otherwise, he will go crazy with his freedom when he moves out."
- "My parents always let me know what they expected from me; what kind of life I should live, what I should do with my friends, etc. My parents always put a lot of trust in me and they gave me freedom to make my own choices. I think they might have limited my freedom if they knew some of the things I did. But, most of my friends got into a lot more trouble than I did and their parents were more strict. I think my parents instilled in me a responsibility for my actions and they let me know that I would disappoint them if I let them down."

Both these young people are telling us in their own way that letting go helps reduce the need for discipline later down the line.

Praying for Your Teens

How easy it is to let other priorities and activities crowd out the time we need to bring the needs of our family to God in prayer. We are all busy as parents; there are so many demands on our time. But this may be the most important "ounce of prevention" of all.

Many of the young people who filled out the survey wrote at length about what advice they would want to give parents about discipline. The most articulate response was from a twenty-year-old Canadian girl who wrote a stirring call to all parents:

Pray for your kids! Have absolutely no confidence in your good intentions or whatever parental qualifications you may have. My parents are both graduates of a highly respected Bible college. My father has a Ph.D. in the behavioral sciences. Both are committed Christians and walk closely with the Lord. Yet despite these apparently foolproof qualifications, they failed to figure out that their oldest child (me) was taking large and frequent doses of various substances such as LSD, PCP, speed, as well as "organics." Perhaps you marvel at my parents' inability to perceive that which should be so obvious; perhaps you marvel at my church's failure to reach out to me as I was being dragged down by the enemy.

If so, marvel even more at the shrewdness and frightening precision of Satan's psychological attacks. They [the attacks] are so subtle and sly that we are defeated without even noticing. The battles will take place in the minds of your children, which despite X years of experience, brilliant education, wondrous qualifications, and your highest hopes, are veritably inaccessible to you. But there is One who has access, and the power to win those battles . . . it is to Him you must make your pleas and entrust your kids.

In this chapter we've looked at things we can do that reduce the need for discipline in the first place. What happens, though, when we realize that our approach to parenting is causing much of the problem? Is it really possible to change our parenting style if we need to?

DISCUSSION QUESTIONS

1. Can you recall any incidents recently when it would have helped to remember that your son or daughter is normal?

2. When your son or daughter reveals a hurt, a problem, or a need, what do you usually do first: give advice, reassure, identify the problem, or reveal yourself?

3. When was the last time you shared a personal struggle with your teenager and asked for prayer?

4. When you were the age your son or daughter is now, what was your self-esteem like? If it needed improving, what would have helped it?

5. Are you praying enough for your family? What stands in your way of a better prayer life?

6. Open your Bible to Lamentations 3:22–24. How does it make you feel that the steadfast love of the Lord never ceases? In what way are His mercies new every morning to you? How does this give you hope as you think about the future and your family?

10

Changing Your
Parenting Style

Our first home in Seattle was a vintage fifties, three-bed-room, one-and-a-half-bath rambler with an unremarkable front yard. My wife and I put up with looking at that ugly real estate for a few years, but finally, *it was time*. The month: early June. The goal: terrace the front yard before baby number three was due to be born in mid-July.

One day we had fifty huge railroad ties delivered. The noise of the winch brought our neighbors to their windows. The next day a massive dump truck brought four heaping loads of dirt from a nearby construction site. This brought the neighbors to their front porches, aghast. "Trust me," I tried to comfort my disbelieving friends, "things always look worse before they look better."

Then the work began. My normal fifty to sixty hours per week at church didn't change, so I got up early in the morning. Instead of going out to run, I went out to dig. As dusk turned to darkness, I could again be seen in the front yard, digging another trench, wheelbarrowing another pile, or wrestling with a timber that weighed more than I did.

July 19 came. In middle evening a neighbor stopped by to admire the work. He cautioned my wife, who did look a little silly moving dirt when she was nine months pregnant. "Hey, you're going to make that baby come out, you're working so hard!"

As the last pile of dirt was being relocated to its proper place, Janet went inside the house; I finished an hour later. We went to the hospital immediately and our third daughter was born ninety minutes later.

Changing our landscape was a lot of work, but as we held our newest daughter and enjoyed the view, we decided it was worth it.

Changing parenting styles can seem like a daunting task. It can be a lot of work. Yet if we hang in there and finish what we start, it will be worth it.

Changing parenting styles has a lot to do with discipline. If we are autocratic or authoritarian, and we hang on to that style as our kids pass the early teen years, we nudge our kids toward rebellion and their peers. They'll reject not only our discipline but other things we try to teach them also. If we are too permissive or ignoring in our style, we run the risk of sentencing our kids to a life of poor self-esteem—which also targets them toward negative peer influences. This also leads to rejection of our discipline, should a situation arise where we feel correction is justified.

If a change to a parenting style that is more productive is in order, we need to keep the benefits firmly in mind.

• *It will benefit our young people.* Remember that discipline is simply one of the many ways we teach as parents. It helps them learn some vital lessons that one cannot transition successfully into adult life without: respect for authority, accountability, and control of impulses. Therefore we want to create an environment where our young people accept, rather than react against, reasonable discipline and correction.

• *It will benefit us as parents as well!* If our home is full of stress and tension, a change of parenting style will begin to make a difference. We will begin to feel a lessening of tension and a sense that God is working in our lives for the better.

Even if your home is a model of proper parenting style and its positive result, become familiar with what is presented here. You may be able to help preclude disaster in another family that you notice spiraling downward.

Changing Styles: Basic Strategy

Tom and Lynda Foster are sitting at the breakfast table. The house is quiet now, but it wasn't a few minutes ago before their teenage son and daughter left for school. It has not been a happy morning.

"I did it again," Tom laments. "When Jim forgot to feed the dog this morning, I treated it like a capital offense. I didn't mean to yell. I didn't mean to be mean; it just came out. Jim's a great kid, yet I know he left here this morning feeling that I hate him."

So as the coffee cools in their mugs, and the syrup dries on their plates, the Fosters wonder, "Can we change the way we treat our kids?"

Yes, they can. And *you* we can change the way you relate to your kids! Later we will look at specific ways to change specific styles. First, however, we need to understand there are some preliminary steps to take.

1. Spend Time in Prayer

Surprise! Well, not really. At least it shouldn't be a surprise that we should pray about our need for change. A major sign of personal growth and spiritual maturity is when we take things to God first. Instead of doing our best and then asking God for a little help with what we can't handle, it is far better to begin with prayer.

"Lord, I don't think I can change my hot temper with my son. I admit I've sinned—against You, against him. I admit I am weak and You are strong. I seem powerless to change, but *You* are powerful."

It takes a strong person to admit weakness. It takes guts to admit failure. Yet so often it is our own repeated failure which drives us to our knees and proper dependence on the Lord.

We should pray specifically about what needs to be changed, but our prayers probably shouldn't start there. We should begin with cultivating a deeper friendship with Jesus Christ. We best set the stage for personal growth and change when we learn to enjoy God in worship and realize He wants to enjoy us. Change occurs in our lives more as an outflow of our deepening relationship with Him than it does out of anything else. When it comes to change, we need to see change in *ourselves* first.

Yet having said all that, we still should pray specifically about our requests. He wants us to, and we come to Him who knows and understands our deepest needs and our deepest hurts.

2. Be Accountable

Be what? Change is much more likely to happen in our lives when we make ourselves accountable. Of course we're accountable to God, yet it helps to have someone on the planet with whom we have shared our failure and to whom we report our progress.

The world knows that setting up an accountability structure goes a long way to encourage positive results. We've all heard the testimonies: "I've lost thirty-four pounds in ten weeks with the Mary Smith Weight Loss Plan. My personal counselor, Shelley, has been wonderful, and I know I will maintain my weight loss with her help."

With whom can we do this?

a. Our spouse. It's logical to begin here. As husband and wife we need to agree on what needs to be changed. This will require some honest communication and joint decision making. Words of encouragement need to be given when progress is seen, and there needs to be understanding and comfort when there is failure. A joint commitment to change can bring a sense of unity and common purpose to a marriage.

Unfortunately, honest communication, joint decision making, and words of affirmation are not part of the repertoire of some marriages. Only one partner may see the need for change. Or both may see the need but lack the communication skills to pull it off.

In the first case, the partner who sees the need for change might need to just begin to change unilaterally, and seek accountability with an understanding friend. In the second case, a few sessions with a good marriage counselor would increase the probability for success. (There is nothing shameful about getting professional help! The stakes are so high, it will be worth the price.)

The single parent will need the understanding support of a close friend or associate.

b. Friend or support group. Tom and Lynda Foster have recently joined one of the fellowship/Bible study groups in their church. It is time for prayer requests and Lynda begins.

"Tom and I really need your prayer and help in something that is happening at home."

"Yeah," Tom continues, "I've realized my temper is really turning our son away from us. It seems like hardly a morning goes by without some kind of blowup. He's sort of irresponsible and it annoys me a lot. My reaction is usually white-hot anger with a raised voice. The Lord has begun to show me how wrong I've been, and I just pray it's not too late to improve. Anyway, could you please pray that in the next week, instead of five morning blowups, maybe it would be only one or two. I don't have the faith to believe this will all be solved in a week, but God only knows how much I long to see at least some progress. I'll report when we meet next week."

Tom and Lynda Foster have taken a major step in making a positive change. They have decided not to do what many Christians seem to do: cover up. Christians shouldn't have problems, right? If we admit we have problems, doesn't it show how bad we are, and then what will all those people think who don't have problems? They will look down at us, won't they? Some probably will; in the church we are awfully good at shooting our own wounded.

Yet with a trusted friend, or in the context of a supportive and honest small group, we can share our failure, our need for prayer, and our need for help.

3. Set Specific Goals

"Improving my parenting style" is a warm fuzzy goal, but it is not specific enough. If we tend to be too lenient, an appropriate goal could be to "require two household chores per week for each of my kids, and hold them responsible for them." If we tend to be too strict, we might determine that the next time a discipline situation arises we will "ask my daughter what she thinks a reasonable response should be—and unless absolutely impossible, follow her suggestion." We will work on setting these types of goals later.

4. Role-play

Write down a couple of bad situations in recent memory and role-play (with your spouse, friend, or support group) a more productive style as a response. Make a game of it; have your spouse rate your efforts.

5. Hold a Family Conference

If you are in agreement with your spouse about what needs to be changed, it's time to have a family conference. Most parents will not find this agenda an easy one, but it will get your son's or daughter's attention, guaranteed!

Family conference proposed agenda:

a. Apologize for your failures as a parent.
b. Acknowledge the pain/suffering/frustration you have caused and ask for their forgiveness.
c. Spell out clearly how and why you hope to change. Share your specific goals if appropriate.
d. Ask for their support, in prayer and encouragement.
e. If your kids are Christians, pray together about the issues that have been raised.

6. Practice Off-the-Wall Behavior

It's very easy to get in a rut. It could be our style of parenting, our daily schedule, the way we think, the food we buy. Often it is very difficult to change something in our lives if we are not accustomed to changing anything.

It can help if we purposely do some things we don't normally do, just to be different. Little things, crazy things, things that will help us—and those around us—believe that we are capable of change.

Don't have a clue? Try these:

a. Serve ice-cream sundaes for supper as the main course.
b. Leave for work ten minutes early and stop at a park to take a walk.
c. Before clearing the table after dinner, go read the paper on the front porch.
d. Write a letter of thanks to your pastor and enclose McDonald's gift certificates for his kids.
e. Sit at a different place at the supper table.
f. Go to the library and check out a book on the city of Rome.

The list can be endless! Try doing a couple of new things a day for a couple of weeks. You'll probably have your family rolling on the floor laughing, but what harm is that? If you have had a family conference, they will understand what you are doing and why. Sure, they may look in the yellow pages under "Psychiatric Evaluation and Intervention," but they probably won't call the funny farm unless you do something that's *major league* off-the-wall. (Quitting your job as an attorney and opening a flower stall on a downtown street corner would probably qualify as major league weird.)

So . . . let your imagination run wild. One caution is in order. This might be so much fun it could become a permanent feature of your family life. When your children are grown, they'll sit around the table at Thanksgiving and smilingly say, "Remember the good old days when Dad wore a flannel shirt to a business meeting?"

These six steps for changing parenting style have been preliminary in nature. Now let's turn to specific actions appropriate to specific styles.

Changing From an Autocratic/Authoritarian Style

1. Definition Review

Back in Chapter 3 we defined the various parenting styles. To be *autocratic* is to not allow our kids to express opinions or make decisions about aspects of their own lives. To be *authoritarian* is not quite so strict; the teenager is allowed to contribute opinions but parents always make the final judgment. Parents who tend toward this style often think in terms of what is the appropriate punishment for a certain action. Raised voices, anger, and the negative words that come so easy when tempers are flaring are all commonly associated with these styles.

Go back to the Parenting Style Questionnaire in Chapter 3 and review your answers to the first five questions. If you answered "usually" to more than three of the questions, your style tends toward autocratic or authoritarian. These styles, especially if associated with low nurturance, produce little more than increasing amounts of resentment, bitterness, and rebellion as our kids go through the teenage years.

2. Appropriate Goals

The parent who is autocratic or authoritarian is the best person to write his or her own specific goals for change. However, if one is not accustomed to writing goals that are actually reachable, help may be needed to get started. Discuss this with your spouse, or brainstorm with a trusted friend who knows your situation. Here are some suggestions which may fit the need:

a. GOAL: *Change my view of discipline, away from punishment and toward a positive teaching method.* Of the eighteen discipline methods mentioned in Chapter 4, list on the next page three that are teaching-oriented.

1.

2.

3.

Mentally replay the last time you punished your teenager. What did your son or daughter need to learn from that situation? Write your answer here:

Visualize the situation again and use one of the methods listed above instead of what you did. How do you think the situation would have turned out differently?

b. GOAL: To reduce the number of times I respond to my kids in anger. Of course there is such a thing as righteous anger. Jesus was angry when He drove out the money changers from the temple (John 2). Unfortunately most of us are much more skilled at carnal hostility than righteous indignation.

Visualize the next likely event in which you would be angry with your son or daughter; write it below in a summary sentence. Then role-play it with your spouse or friend, using a more positive discipline method than what you would normally use and without anger.

(Now this is work, right? We never said it would be easy! We can't change our parenting style by reading a chapter of this book or any book. It will take practice and patience. Don't give up!)

Prayerfully study the chart shown on the following page. Take the time to look up the Scriptures included, and consider how they might apply to you.

RIGHTEOUS INDIGNATION AND CARNAL HOSTILITY

	Righteous Indignation	Carnal Hostility	Biblical References
Direction	Toward sin or toward a non-Christian but never toward a son (Christian)	Toward anything or anybody that upsets us	Ps. 7:11 Gal. 5:19–21
Purpose	To right a wrong (or) To promote holiness	To gain revenge (or) To protect self-image	Rom. 12:17–21
Attitude	Exists with love	Exists alone	I Cor. 13:4–7 Lam. 3:33
Method	Slow and controlled	Rapid and impulsive	Jas. 1:19–21 Prov. 16:32
Result In Child	Increased respect for the parent	Increased hostility toward the parent	Prov. 15:1 Eph. 6:4
Result in Parent	Satisfaction for Christian concern	Relief from expressing hostility, followed by guilt over losing temper	

Taken from *Help! I'm a Parent!* by S. Bruce Narramore. Copyright © 1972 by The Zondervan Corporation, p. 140. Used by permission.

Think back to the last week. How many times were you angry at your teenagers?

Write your goal for the coming week, and share it with your spouse or friend.

c. GOAL: To show my kids more respect by asking their opinion and listening to their advice. Think of a project in the yard or around the house. Or, think ahead to your next family vacation. Go to your teenager and ask for his or her opinion or advice. Express gratitude for that opinion and incorporate it, if at all possible. If it is not possible, explain without anger or annoyance why it won't work out.

Do this at least once a week for the next four weeks. Record here your teenager's suggestions:

Week 1:

Week 2:

Week 3:

Week 4:

d. GOAL: To be more nurturing. Fill in the following chart concerning the number of times you . . .

	Did This Last Week	Plan to Do It Next Week
1. Hug or touch my kids.	___	___
2. Be available to listen to my kids' problems.	___	___
3. Express appreciation.	___	___
4. Affirm my kids when they do something well.	___	___
5. Spend one-on-one time with them.	___	___

3. Prayer and Practice

As recommended in the basic strategy, follow through with specific prayer and setting up an accountability structure. Talk about it in your family. Role-play with your spouse or friend the situations in which you have failed. You can even role-play with your teenagers!

Changing From a Permissive/Ignoring Style

1. Definition Review

To be *permissive* is to allow the teenager to make his or her own decisions. Parental preferences may receive consideration in the decision making, but abiding by parental preference is not an essential expectation. *Ignoring* is a style in which the parent shows no interest in the behavior of the teenager and plays virtually no role in guiding the behavior.

The permissive/ignoring style, done without much nurturance, produces young people who are insecure and have low self-esteem. (See Chapter 3.) They are so geared toward getting support from their peers that any attempt at discipline would normally be rejected.

Of course a permissive style with good nurturance will be the logical end point at the end of adolescence. In fact, 63 percent of the survey respondents indicated this was the style their parents used when they were in late adolescence, and it was successful.

2. *Appropriate Goals*

If your tendency is to be permissive or ignoring, you are the best one to write specific goals. You will need to remember that, especially in early adolescence, it is appropriate to provide loving but firm guidelines on some behavior. Regaining influence in this area should be your primary focus.

Here are some suggested goals to start your thinking:

a. GOAL: To take a more active interest in my son's or daughter's life. In casual conversation over the next few days, find out your teenager's "favorites." (Record below.)

TV show:

Recreational activity:

Food:

Music:

Friends:

In the coming week plan something you will do with your teenager that has to do with one of the favorites (e.g., go out for the favorite food; watch the TV show together). What will you do?

   b. GOAL: To set a guideline that will help my son or daughter see that I love them very much. If possible, choose an event or area that is still in the future for your teenager. Examples could include: dating, getting a driver's license, getting a part-time job, going to a summer camp, or going on a short-term missions project. Agree together what it will take for them to be granted freedom to choose in that area.

   Here's how one family used this approach:

> Son, you're almost fifteen now and I want you to know your mom and I are really excited about your getting older. We see so many good things in your life and so much potential. I'm sure you are really looking forward to getting your driver's license. Well, we are too. You can well imagine that it takes a lot of maturity and responsibility to drive a car.
>
> In the coming year, if you are able to be responsible in your chores around the house and show a good attitude about it, you can get your license the day you turn sixteen and you'll have limited use of the family car. How about that?

   Notice this "speech" is filled with affirmation and positive expectation. It communicates love but that there are guidelines too.

   In the area you've chosen, write your own speech, or put it in letter format. Go over it with your spouse or friend.

3. Prayer and Practice

Prayerfully write your own goals and follow the basic strategy outlined above. Report your progress readily to whomever you are accountable.

Changing your parenting style is work, but it's worth it. We've tried here to move from styles on either end of the influence/control continuum toward the center—that is, toward the democratic or equalitarian style described in Chapter 3. If we are trying to change from autocratic to democratic, our efforts will probably be greeted with cheers from our teenagers. Our efforts to move from permissive to democratic might not be so favorably received.

If we have lost control of our kids, or never really had it in the first place, how do we get control in a positive way? Sure, we can carry a big stick around the house, but realistically and as Christians, how do we actually pull it off without sending our kids out the door? We now turn our attention in that direction.

DISCUSSION QUESTIONS

1. Do you and your spouse feel there is a need to change your parenting style? Why or why not?

2. The author states that Christians are very good at covering up their weaknesses and family problems. If you agree, why?

3. Go ahead and role-play at least one situation that creates heat between you and your teenager.

4. Are you in a rut? How easy is it for you to change? Do you have a need to show a little off-the-wall behavior to get things rolling?

5. Open your Bible to 2 Corinthians 3:4–6, 18. According to these verses, when we see a need to change in our lives, what part does God play and what part do we play in the change? If we are resting in Him for the strength to make the change, why does that give us confidence?

11

Regaining Control —————◇

Ever tried to fix a leaky bathtub faucet? Bathroom plumbing was not one of the courses available when I went to seminary, but I'm bold enough to try just about anything when it comes to home repairs. Our second home in Seattle was a vintage 1913 "fixer." It may have been wiser or more merciful to just bulldoze it and start all over again, but we chose to try to fix it up.

The night I tried to fix the bathtub faucets, I had allotted about one hour for the job. I thought it would take a half hour, but experience had taught me to double the time I expected things to take. The project ended up taking twenty frustrating hours, stretched over five days, and costing about $60.00. I learned about tools and valve parts that I never knew existed. Aside from raising my "home improvement time estimate" calculation method, I learned one extremely valuable lesson: with plumbing, one size does not fit all.

One Size Does Not Fit All

As with plumbing, so with parenting. One method, one approach, does not work equally well in different families.

Let's get acquainted briefly with three families. The parents are facing similar situations in that they all realize they need to regain control, but the similarity ends there.

• *The Cordozas* have a fifteen-year-old son, Juan, and a fourteen-year-old daughter, René. Both are strong willed and have pretty much ruled the house since they were old enough to walk. The parents realize now they are headed for serious problems in the future if they can't somehow get a handle on what's happening and how to deal with it.

• *Lynn Simmonds* has been a single parent for a decade. At 6'2" and 200 pounds, her seventeen-year-old son, Peter, dwarfs her. For him, "home" is a place to eat and sleep. He makes no effort to contribute to cleaning; in fact, Lynn rarely sees him—only the messes he leaves behind. His attitude is belligerent to her much of the time.

• *The Kellys* thought they were pretty good parents until their daughter Susan hit middle adolescence. Their son, Jack, is a year older than Susan and has been no problem whatsoever in his teenage years. Susan, on the other hand, is fourteen going on twenty. She wants to stay out late, sleep late, has marginal interest in school, and helps around the house only when the Kellys threaten her or beg.

How shall we advise these parents? Take a six-year vacation in Australia and come back after their kids turn twenty-one? Appealing, perhaps, but not practical.

Let's walk them through six steps that they each can take in common, and then see from there how their action steps will differ.

Six Steps to Insight

We already know that parenting and teaching through discipline is work. We saw in Chapter 10 that changing our parenting style is work. Well, it's work to regain control as well! Answering these questions may not be easy, but it is necessary if progress is to be made.

1. How Bad Is Your Problem?

Realistically appraise your situation. Most of us are not capable of being objective about our own family. Talk this one through with good friends or a support group. What specific behaviors or attitudes do you see in your teenager that give you cause for concern?

As our three families think about this, it isn't hard for them to identify where their kids are at. Let's listen in.

> *Cordozas:* "Both Juan and René are rebellious. They won't talk with us, we know they've lied, and all they want to do is be with their friends. We don't like the crowd they're beginning to hang around with either."
>
> *Lynn:* "Peter is aggressive, if not criminal. He thinks that I owe him—that life owes him—a free ride. He has no goals, no purpose, just day-to-day highs."
>
> *Kellys:* "Susan is pretty good but beginning to change. It really frightens us to see the downward path she could be on."

2. When Did It Get This Way?

Answering this question may provide insight later when we consider what to do to regain control. Think back: when did it first become obvious to you that there was a problem?

> *Cordozas:* "We began losing control around fourth grade. Sure, Juan and René sort of obeyed us then, but when they hit junior high they both gravitated toward the rock 'n' roll crowd—with the tattered clothes and heavy metal music."
>
> *Lynn:* "It was actually okay through half of junior high. In eighth grade, though, Peter had an amazing growth spurt. Once he was taller than I and obviously stronger, he began asserting himself more and more around the house. He knew there was nothing I could do."
>
> *Kellys:* "It was just six months ago. Susan was always more mature than her peers, but then she started being super aware of her body, clothing, and guys."

3. Why Did It Get This Way?

There may or may not be an easy answer here. Much of it has to do with the parenting style we've been using. As we have seen in Chapter 3, a combination of low nurturance with a high autocratic style, or low nurturance with an ignoring style, will especially produce disastrous results.

Much of it has to do with the kind of teenager our young person is. A classic second-born will by nature be insecure and "require" peer approval in the extreme. We may have to admit our own lack of ability in communication. There may be many contributing factors. Try to write them down.

> *Cordozas:* "We are quiet and shy by nature. Neither my wife nor I speak up for ourselves or what we think. I think our kids realized that we weren't going to discipline them and that kind of gave them the green light to just do and be what they wanted.
>
> "We don't feel very successful with life in general. That we're failing with Juan and René is quite honestly how we feel about a lot of things. If I had to classify our parenting style, I guess we're permissive with not much nurture."
>
> *Lynn:* "I wish I had not lost touch with him. It was so frustrating when Peter wouldn't talk with me. There was a period in junior high when I yelled at him a lot, but then I just gave up. I had an extended illness, and it was all I could do to go to work and barely survive keeping up the house. There just wasn't time or energy to 'be there for him' when he needed it. It seems it's too late now."
>
> *Kellys:* "Maybe we were just blind to the potential problems. We saw Jack turn out so nicely, and we just assumed Susan would too. We see now she's a typical Type 2. Had we realized that, we could have tried harder to build her self-esteem and make her feel we respected her more."

4. At What Stage of Adolescence Is Your Teenager Now?

We saw in Chapters 4–8 the profound differences this makes. What may work with a thirteen-year-old will probably not work with an eighteen-year-old.

Cordozas: "Juan and René are both middle adolescents."
Lynn: "Peter's definitely in late adolescence."
Kellys: "Susan is in middle adolescence."

5. Where Are You in Terms of Being a Friend to Your Son/ Daughter?

We saw in Chapter 9 how important it is to have a relationship with our kids. Our efforts to regain control will probably not be seen as a gesture of friendship by our kids, but if the situation stabilizes in the home, we will want to improve the friendship factor if at all possible.

Cordozas: "We've never been friends with our kids. We hardly even know them now, and they don't know us."
Lynn: "We're at war most of the time."
Kellys: "We still have a relationship, though it is strained at times."

6. What Are Your Bottom-Line Goals?

We don't go to the effort to regain control or influence our kids just for the fun of it. Will we be content to stop abusive behavior and then propose to be quite permissive with them in other areas as a trade-off? Do we want to see our family be a model of Christian community? Is our goal to see the kids help around the house?

Focusing our goals is essential to prayer and planning as we begin implementation.

Cordozas: "It's hard to believe that anything can change. I guess we'd want to see our kids respect our authority, but we realize we've got to get better at communication so they know what to expect. Sure we'd want our family to be a model Christian family, but that seems like fantasy now. Maybe we'd have the faith to believe that could happen if we saw a little progress in the next few months."
Lynn: "This one's easy: I want to reduce the tension level in our home between Peter and me. I want us to support and understand each other instead of being adversaries."

Kellys: "We'd like to figure out how to motivate Susan to make right decisions and be closer to the Lord."

A Seventh Step—Action

Custom Made

In addition to prayer, what are my logical next steps? Here is where one size does *not* fit all. We have seen in Chapters 4–8 how different methods of discipline work differently with certain kinds of young people. Our action plan must be tailor-made to fit our own situation and the goals we have in mind.

For example, with an early adolescent, the threat of restrictions is enforceable. With a late adolescent, it generally is not. Similarly, the reward of going to a special sports or recreation camp six months later may be a real motivation to a thirteen-year-old girl who can "think about a thought." As you recall from Chapter 4, this mental skill begins much earlier in girls than boys. It means that they can connect in their minds that action now will have a consequence later down the line, and will change behavior accordingly. A thirteen-year-old boy, however, may not have this skill, and the promise of anything more than a week in the future, no matter how wonderful, will have no impact on current behavior.

Generally, the older the young person, the better long-term consequences are understood, either good or bad.

We will keep in mind also that, while all young people have similar needs (self-esteem, respect, and acceptance), what will develop this in the young person will need to be custom tailored.

A Crucial Skill for Regaining Control[1]

Before seeing some sample action plans, we need to consider a communication strategy that can be used profitably with just about any age young person. Let's call it, "getting our point across."

How do we usually communicate our wishes to our young people?

Dad: Mary, it's your turn to clean up the kitchen tonight.
Mary: I'll do it later.
Dad: (slightly louder voice) You'll do it now.
Mary: I'm going to make a couple of phone calls, and then I'll get to it. Get off my back. I had to do it for Tom last week. Get him to do it if you want it done now.
Dad: (louder still) I said do it now or you'll be grounded!

These exchanges don't help digest the evening meal, do they? We need to learn to express our desires without raising our voices, getting off the subject, or backing down. Let's play that last scenario again.

Dad: It's your night for the kitchen, Mary; please do it now.
Mary: I'll do it later.
Dad: I understand that you have other things you'd rather do, but I've asked you to do it now.
Mary: I've got a couple of phone calls to make, and I'm real busy. Why don't you get Tom do it?
Dad: I understand you've got things to do. But I've asked you to do it now.
Mary: Get off my back! You're nagging me.
Dad: I know you feel this is nagging, but I have asked you to do it now.
Mary: Okay; okay. See, I'm starting.
Dad: Thank you. I appreciate that.

Or this . . .

Mary: You're so demanding. I hate this. I'm not going to do it.
Dad: I understand this feels hard to you and that you don't like it, but I've asked you to do it now. If you don't, your mom is going to go on strike. You're a busy girl; wouldn't it seem better just to clean up the kitchen as scheduled, instead of having to do all your own cooking and laundry?

Mary: She wouldn't.

Dad: You may not think she would, but we've discussed this
and I know she will. I've asked you to clean up the kitchen
or face a strike. Take your pick.

Question: Does Mary understand what her father wants
her to do and when? No doubt about that one! He has not
been distracted or deflected but has stood his ground.

This technique produces some stress and tension initially,
particularly if the young person is strong willed. However,
if the parents stick to it and follow through on the Parental
Strike (or whatever reinforcement measure is chosen), the
parent is likely to come out the winner. When the young
person has obeyed, then a liberal dose of nurturance is in
order.

Dad: Mary, I know we had some stress earlier in the evening,
and I realize I made things uncomfortable for you. But I
thank you for cooperating. You are a wonderful daughter
and I love you very much.

Perhaps suggesting a mutually enjoyable activity, like
scheduling a time to go out for pizza, would be another
reinforcer.

This communication approach takes a permissive or ignoring parent and makes him or her authoritarian *temporarily.* Nurturance, when obedience occurs, is crucial to its
success. While an authoritarian approach may not be generally the best way to raise a kid, it may be needed to regain
control or influence in a situation in sad need of help. It
works because the young person finally figures out that the
hassle of obeying is much less than the hassle of always
hearing "I understand you feel . . . but I've asked you. . . . "

Some parents reading this may have used a similar method
a decade earlier when it came to potty training. *Potty Training in One Day*[2] may seem like a fantasy title to some, but it
works. My wife and I read the book in time for our second
and third daughters. Both were successfully potty trained in
one day using the plan suggested. And what is that plan?

Essentially the parent in that twelve-hour day makes it much less hassle for the kid to use the potty than to make a mistake.

This communication strategy follows the same principle. It clearly spells out what you expect as a parent, and eventually makes obedience seem like the easiest response.

What if the parent is already autocratic or authoritarian? There are three major differences in the approach just explained that set it aside from the blind autocratic or authoritarian style:

1. It focuses on a specific behavior and, without raised voice or anger, makes the parental desire explicitly clear.
2. It is dedicated to not letting the conversation get distracted or deflected off the issue in question.
3. There are real discipline consequences involved that will be experienced by the noncomplying young person.

Three Examples of Action Plans

Let's take a look at the action plans decided upon by our three sample families. We have already walked through the first six steps together. Remember, different discipline methods are explained fully in Chapter 4. Be thinking about what your own action plan could be for the situation you face in your own home.

Cordozas' Action Plan

A: Parenting style.

Needs changing from *permissive* to *democratic*. Begin following suggestions in Chapter 10.

B: Action needed to accomplish goals.

Call a Family Council as described in Chapter 10, and present the following:

- List of possible chores around the house.
- Benefits and rewards of those chores successfully done.
- Let Juan and René each choose three.

C: Communication strategy.

Use the communication strategy between "Dad" and "Mary" described earlier. Role-play with your spouse to become used to the technique of acknowledging Juan's and René's excuses or protests ("I understand you think...") but remaining firm (" ... but I've asked you to ...").

D: Last-resort discipline.

If the kids don't cooperate, suspend phone privileges and remove all the extensions in the house except the one in the parents' bedroom until cooperation is complete. (The Cordozas know their kids greatly value their phone extensions.)

E: Nurturance plan.

1. To communicate love: say so, touch, give small surprise gift.

2. To communicate acceptance: spend time together on something the kids like. Mrs. Cordoza will take René shopping in Dallas (a hundred miles away). Mr. Cordoza will take Juan on an ATV trek through the hills.

3. To communicate respect: Mr. Cordoza will consult Juan's opinion on purchase of a new used car. Mrs. Cordoza will consult René on kitchen remodeling.

F: Maintenance.

Set up a weekly Family Council.

Lynn Simmonds' Action Plan

A: Parenting style.

Parenting style doesn't really need to change. Lynn has always tried to be *democratic*. When she had the extended illness she was *ignoring*, but has tried since then to be democratic in style.

B: Action needed to accomplish goals.

1. Since Peter usually comes home after Lynn goes to bed and gets up after she leaves for work, a notice will be posted on his bedroom door:

To: Peter

From: Mom

Dear son, you know I love you very much. Yet you also know I am very frustrated by your attitude toward me and your unwillingness to help around the house. I realize I have hurt myself and you by not taking steps to get this issue resolved earlier; for that I apologize.

I hereby call for a family meeting tomorrow night at 10:00 P.M. If you miss that meeting you will find no food in the house the next day. You can pay for your own groceries. I have made alternative meal arrangements for myself which I will use, if necessary.

If you are destructive to my property or if I find anything stolen, you will come home to find your things on the front porch and the locks changed. I have contacted a locksmith who can do the job in less than an hour. All I need to do is call.

At this family meeting we will negotiate a contract for house rules and chores. Also, I would very much like to be your friend, and not just the nonperson I am now. I don't know if it's possible but I would like to talk about it.

It's your choice, Peter. I hope to see you at 10:00 P.M. tomorrow night.

2. Contract negotiation.
3. Weekly list of chores and in-hours.

C and D: Communication strategy/Last-resort discipline.

Not really needed, since the contract will already say that he's out if he doesn't comply.

E: Nurturance plan.

1. To communicate love: To come to the meeting with a present for her son—the latest issue and a subscription to *Car and Driver*, something Peter's been wanting.

2. To communicate acceptance: To try to listen to him without interrupting or put-downs during and after the meeting.

3. To communicate respect: This will be a challenge considering how bad the situation already is. Lynn's plan: To admire his car, ask for a ride, and generally show an interest in his obvious skill in this area.

F: Maintenance.

The negotiated contract will call for a certain number of supper meals eaten together. Lynn is hoping for three per week. (She'll state five first but "back down" to three.) After a time of personal prayer, she will come to each meal primed to listen and show care and acceptance.

Kellys' Action Plan

A: Parenting style.

The Kellys' parenting style needs to change from *permissive* to *democratic*. They will follow the specific strategy outlined in Chapter 10.

B: Action needed to accomplish goals.

Actions are implied in changing parenting styles and beginning the communication strategy. Action is also implied in the nurturance plan.

C: Communication strategy.

Use the communication strategy between "Dad" and "Mary" described earlier. Role-play with your spouse or a friend, if possible, to become used to the technique of acknowledging your teenager's excuses or protests ("I understand you think...") but remaining firm ("...but I've asked you to...").

D: Last-resort discipline.

If Susan doesn't cooperate, employ a Parental Strike, e.g., Dad: stop chauffeuring; Mom: stop laundry.

E: Nurturance plan.

1. To communicate love: This will be hard, since Susan is such a monster much of the time. When she is nice, however, the Kellys have decided to show extra care in listening and affirming her. They will also begin being more verbal in telling her they love her and appreciate her contribution to the family.

2. To communicate acceptance: They know she loves horseback riding and skiing. Mom will offer to take her and a friend riding soon. Dad will offer to take her and a friend skiing when the season comes. They will also look for things that do not cost money that they can do with their daughter just to spend time with her. (Example: Mom will sit down with Susan once a week late at night just to listen to the song that happens to be on the radio station she's listening to. Though Mrs. Kelly might not like the music or the content, she will not comment negatively on it until such time as communication channels between them are not so tenuous.

3. To communicate respect: Will ask for Susan's opinion in the upcoming elections. Will ask for her opinions on how school could be more interesting and take her suggestions to the vice-principal unless her ideas are completely unfeasible.

F: Maintenance.

Mr. and Mrs. Kelly will spend time together on Sunday night evaluating the previous week and discussing the coming week. Changes and modifications will be made as needed.

All three of our families are not so naive as to think that every last thing they have set out to do will turn out as they expect. Yet, with prayer and God's strength and working on it, they do expect that these things will begin to make a difference. We notice that in each case, regaining control doesn't just happen. It's an intervention—with all the work and stress that an intervention implies.

It's Your Turn Now

Take the time now to prayerfully chart out your own preliminary information and action steps. Make a photocopy of the chart if you have more than one young person. If you have a close friend or a support group, bring it to them for feedback, comments, and prayer support.

1. How bad is my problem? (Describe.)

2. When did it get this way?

3. Why did it get this way?

4. At what stage of adolescence is my teenager now?

5. Where am I in terms of being a friend to my son/daughter?

6. What are my bottom-line goals?

7. In addition to prayer, what are my logical next steps?

    A. Parenting style need changing?

    B. Action needed? If yes, what?

    C. Communication strategy.

    D. Last-resort discipline.

    E. Nurturance plan.

        To communicate love:

        To communicate acceptance:

        To communicate respect:

    F. Maintenance plan.

So, you're beginning to turn things around. You feel you're making progress, or at least are on the verge of making progress. What do you do when you hear "bad news" about your kid from a neighbor, sibling, or friend? Reacting wrongly can mean disaster. Read on to discover ways to handle bad news.

DISCUSSION QUESTIONS

1. Are you facing a situation where you need to regain control with a son or daughter? If so, walk through the six steps to insight, pages 168–172.

2. In your own words, what is the "communication strategy" described on pages 172–175?

3. Determine and share your specific plan from the last two pages of the chapter with a friend or support group.

4. Open your Bible to James 1:1–5. How are you doing at "counting it joy" when you face family problems? In what way do you need His wisdom as you develop a plan to regain control?

12

Handling Bad News _____ ◆

A trapper living in Alaska loved his rugged and independent life. His cabin was far from town. But almost as much as he loved the wildness, he loved his German shepherd. This faithful dog was a perfect companion.

In time, however, he became lonely for more human companionship. His visits to town became more frequent, and eventually he married a wonderful girl who was a rugged individualist like himself. They moved back to the cabin and enjoyed their new life together.

They were both excited as eventually she was about to give birth to their first child, even though it meant moving into town temporarily. During delivery, however, severe complications developed and in that small town there were no specialized medical personnel—only one doctor who did his best to save the life of both mother and child. He succeeded with the child, but he did not succeed with the mother, who bled to death holding her new baby girl in her arms as her husband watched helplessly.

Not many have known the pain and despair experienced by that man, yet as the days turned to weeks he began to be increasingly grateful for his baby daughter and what she represented. His German shepherd lay at his feet in the evening as he held his daughter. Many times he would cry, but his love for his daughter and his four-legged companion deepened.

After six months he felt able to move back to his cabin and resume the life he loved. He ran his trap line with his rifle at night while his dog stayed behind with his sleeping baby.

One morning as light dawned he was walking down the hill toward the cabin and could see that the door was open. He dropped his pelts, ran into the cabin, and was aghast at what he saw. There was blood all over and around the crib. He ran over to the crib and saw his limp daughter covered with caked blood. In the corner of the room he heard a whimpering sound, and saw his German shepherd, also covered in blood. "You killed her!" he screamed as he fired three quick rounds into the head and heart of his dog, killing him instantly.

The shots startled his daughter, who began to cry. He ran to the crib and on closer examination found that under all that blood there was not one scratch on her. And then his eyes caught a glimpse of something else in the room, beyond the crib . . . a dead bobcat, also covered in blood. And then he realized . . . his dog, which he had loved so much and whom he had just blown to pieces, had an hour before saved his daughter's life.[1]

Sometimes we parents are pretty good at doing something similar. We get some bad news from our teenagers— or from someone else about our teenagers—and *before we know the whole story* we come at them with guns blazing. Not literally, of course, but our words can be lethal weapons.

Face it, we *are* going to get bad news from or about our teenagers at some point or another. It's not a question of "if," only a question of "when and what." The specific situation might be a slight altercation or a major crisis, but bad news is going to come.

So how do we handle it? What do we do? How do we react when it hits us?

Different Sources, Different Degrees of Seriousness, Different Reactions

Different Sources

There are three ways bad news can come to us about our kids.

- *We discover it ourselves.* Mrs. Miller is doing her sixteen-year-old son a favor, she thinks. He's been very responsible in doing his own laundry during the last half of the year. But she knows he's got a hectic week with schoolwork, basketball, and the youth group choir presentation coming up, so she's done his laundry for him today and in putting his socks away she discovers four issues of *Penthouse* in his drawer.

- *Someone else gives us the bad news.* "Mr. Daniels? This is Pastor Ron. Jim is all right, but we found two bottles of wine in his duffel bag. Troy and Larry also had some along. I need to ask you to drive to the retreat center and pick Jim up. How soon do you think you can come?"

- *Our kids break the news to us.* "Hello, Mom?" Lisa plaintively asks. "I'm sorry to bother you at work but I need your help. I was with Julie at the mall after school and she got caught shoplifting. I'm at the police station and they won't let me leave without a parent."

Degree of Seriousness

Bad news not only comes to us from different sources but in different degrees of seriousness as well.

The bad news might be a flunked test, a friendship gone bad, lost keys, a broken window, a traffic ticket, or a dented fender. Any of these can be a crisis to the young person and parent. However, there's another level of unhappy news that most would admit produces a crisis no matter how you look at it: drug use, drunkenness, pregnancy, homosexuality, running away, expulsion from school, or trouble with the law.

Different Reactions

Kids are certainly very different in how they handle it when they bring the bad news or become aware that you know what's up.

• *Some kids are defensive.* Mrs. Miller's son, upon finding out that his mom has discovered his personal stash of pornography, may retort, "Sure, I like it. I'm old enough to make my own decisions. At least I don't see prostitutes like some of the guys do."

• *Some are rationalizers.* As Mr. Daniels drives Jim home from the retreat he might hear a speech like this: "I told Pastor Ron it wasn't mine. Troy had asked me to carry some of it for him so it wouldn't be so noticeable. I wasn't going to drink any; I was just glad he had come on the retreat because the speaker was going to be so good."

• *Some are criers.* Lisa might burst into tears the moment her mom walks through the door of the police station.

• *Others are bargainers.* "Well, Dad, I realize a reckless driving ticket is not a laughing matter, but I know you've told me what you drove like when you were sixteen and how many tickets you got. If you want, I'll not drive the car to school for a couple weeks; I can ride with Steve. But of course, I'll need the car to get to work and go out with Sue."

• *Others actually have a biblical reaction.* "Mom, I realize I was wrong in being so careless with your keys. I'm very sorry. Please, I need your forgiveness. I don't want anything to come between us."

Parents have different reactions, as well. As the bad news breaks upon us, we begin to form and show our own response. How we respond as parents will make a huge difference in how our eventual discipline will be received.

Phase 1: Damage Control

Damage Control With You

If we, as Christian parents, are deepening our walk with God and letting His Word affect our thinking and our actions, we have astonishing resources with which to cope with the bad news that comes our way. Consider these certainties and their impact as we try to process the information we have just received:

God is bigger than any problem, crisis, or situation that we face. He is sovereign, He understands and knows. He is our refuge, and we have solid comforting words from the Word:

> Fear not, for I have redeemed you; I have summoned you by name; you are mine. When you pass through the waters, I will be with you; and when you pass through the rivers, they will not sweep over you. When you walk through the fire, you will not be burned; the flames will not set you ablaze. For I am the LORD, your God, the Holy One of Israel, your Savior.
>
> Isaiah 43:1b-3a

Sometimes the crises we face with our kids seem like swollen rivers or a scorching fire. Yet we know we are never alone.

Bad things happen to good people—but that's okay because God can use any situation for good. It rains on the good guys as well as the bad guys, right? One pastor's wedding prayer includes the words, "Lord, we know they will escape none of the problems of life." Some parents might say that having a teenager in the house is one major draining problem. We know God can take the bad things that happen in our family and begin to work good instead.

Do we love God? Are we called according to His purpose? Then Romans 8:28 is a comforting promise: "And we know that in all things God works for the good of those who love him, who have been called according to his purpose."

Sure, it may take awhile to see the good in the disaster we currently face, but in time, we will.

There is an experience of God that comes only when we have a broken heart. The ministry of a broken heart is the theme of David Swartz's book, *Dancing with Broken Bones*.[2] There's no doubt that parenting teenagers can produce ample times when our hearts are broken in disappointment and grief. Yet, we know that for those who turn to God there is a richness of relationship with Him that is not experienced at other times.

These thoughts and convictions can form part of the worldview into which bad news intrudes itself. It doesn't necessarily lessen the pain, shock, or shame, but it does provide a framework in which we begin to process what has happened. Now what about external processing?

Damage Control With Your Teenager

Our outward reaction to bad news is somewhat determined by our parenting style.[3]

Parents who are *permissive* or *ignoring* in their approach are likely to deny that a problem exists or avoid dealing with it. They are avoiders or appeasers. If the Millers (in the previously mentioned situation where Mrs. Miller found a copy of *Penthouse* in her son's drawer) were permissive and/or ignoring, they might amaze us with their reaction—or lack of it. The Millers might register a weak protest about their son's pornography stash but make no effort to communicate on a deep level about the issue of morality, exploitation, godly thinking, etc.

If Mr. Daniels were permissive/ignoring, he might not question Jim's claim that the wine wasn't his and he wasn't going to have any. He might even criticize the youth pastor for being unfair and untrusting.

Lisa's parents would accept her story that she was just along with a shoplifting friend and not give it another thought if they were permissive/ignoring.

It is good for us to trust our teenagers, but we must caution ourselves to not be too gullible. Kids are good at deception, and they admit it. Several mentioned this in my survey. A twenty-year-old girl from Canada wrote: "I was not overtly rebellious . . . [but] . . . I did develop more and more elaborate ways of deceiving them and doing my own thing, despite their 'discipline.'"

Parents who are more *authoritarian* may explode upon hearing bad news. They want to punish their son or daughter immediately, and there will probably be no opportunity given to hear the teenager's side of the story. It is not hard to imagine what a strict authoritarian response would be in the scenarios presented by the Millers, Daniels, and with Lisa.

The authoritarian response, especially if it includes Yelling and Threatening, may escalate the crisis to a real family fight. On the other hand, it may drive the errant young person to being outwardly compliant while inwardly hardening his or her heart against the parents and eventually against God. This attitude of inner rebellion was mentioned by many survey respondents who reported their parents were also very strict.

The best response to bad news is generally given by parents who are more *democratic* or *equalitarian* in their style. These parents are very concerned about the poor choices their kids make, but they get the facts straight before decisions about discipline are considered. If, after all the facts are in, discipline is still warranted, these parents may involve the teenager in deciding the nature of the discipline or its severity. One thing is sure: they will *explain* the what and why of the consequences.

The desire for explanation was an oft-repeated theme in the surveys. Kids see it as crucial to successful discipline. One twenty-year-old girl from Florida wrote at length about her advice for parents.

> Don't be naive, don't think your kid is perfect. Don't expect perfection. . . . Don't lecture and tell your child how much more you know than he or she knows—they don't want to hear it, and it's certainly not going to do any good. Choose the way you discipline by how much good it will do the child, *not* what it will do for you. . . . Give them a chance at everything, but don't give them chance after chance. Make sure they are aware of where you stand or how you feel about issues, but let them make choices for themselves. . . .

If you punish your kid, explain *what* he did wrong, *why* it was wrong, and *what* you expect. Then have them tell you [what they've learned].

Phase 2: The Aftermath

We move now from our internal beliefs regarding "bad times" and our initial outward reactions. Time passes . . . in the process we may choose an appropriate discipline (see Chapters 4–8) and talk through its specific application. If the offense was serious enough, more may need to be done to help heal the wounds created by the crisis at hand.

Two Vital Questions

If we still have any kind of communication or relationship base with our teenager, one of the best approaches is to wait for a good time to talk. In a relaxed setting, simply ask the first question: *"What are you learning in this?"*

As parents we may want to tell them what they should learn by their bad choices. We may have our lecture all organized in our minds and even mentally we may have delivered our speech. Yet we open the door to communication and invite the personal growth of our young person by this simple but probing question.

Lisa's mom spoke with both the police and the store security personnel. She learned what she feared was true: her daughter was shoplifting, too, and had been for the last couple of months. They negotiated the discipline of Community Service for four Saturday mornings, where her dad and Lisa would go to a local food bank and help bag rice and beans in the back room for a couple of hours. It actually turned into a very special time for father and daughter. On the way home from their third trip her dad asked the question:

"So dear, what are you learning from this experience?"
"Plenty, Dad, plenty."
"I'm listening."

"For one thing, I'm going to choose my friends more carefully. Jennifer really pressured me into shoplifting with her. She said I was chicken, and that if I was her friend I'd do it with her. You know what?"

"What?"

"True friends don't do that."

"I won't argue with that. What else?"

"I realize now that when you do wrong, and do it repeatedly, the guilt goes away, but so does the thrill. I was content at first with just little stuff, but then I wanted to get more expensive and better stuff. I also learned that the thrill isn't worth it when you're sitting in a police station."

This conversation isn't over, but we get the idea that Lisa is learning a great deal from her experience. She is much wiser for it.

A second vital question, again appropriate for a relaxed setting: *"What difference would a closer relationship with God have made here?"* Kids don't like to be preached at. If your son or daughter is a Christian, and the Holy Spirit is working in his or her life, some spiritual lessons may be learned in the crisis too. This question may open the door to further insight and restoration.

Comforting the Hurting Young Person

Certainly not all bad news results in a hurting teenager. The shock of a C grade instead of an A wears off quickly and life goes on. Other kids will continue to be rebellious, defiant, and hard-hearted in the aftermath of a crisis. They don't want comfort—they want to rule the universe!

But other young people will benefit from help beyond what we've already discussed. Kevin Huggins, in his book, *Parenting Adolescents,*[4] suggests three additional things we can do to help.

1. Enter your teen's pain. Realize that it was not circumstances that caused your teenager to make a bad decision, but his or her heart that did. If this is true, the wise parent will try to understand at a deep level how a son or daughter really feels about self, about life, about the family. What need was the young person trying to fill that resulted in the misbehavior? What hurt was it?

The Millers' son was feeling inferior to his peers athletically. His body was not as strong and developed as many of the other guys. He was retreating into a world of sexual fantasy and conquest, where he was the one these lovely girls admired.

Jim liked to drink because it relieved the boredom and stress he felt at school during the week. He had come to depend on at least one drunken binge on the weekend. It was not going to be easy to pull that off on a church retreat, but he and his friends had their plans carefully laid.

Lisa was desperate for friendship. She wanted to feel needed and accepted. Moving from out of town last year was especially hard on her, and she hadn't yet found a close group of friends.

Here we as parents are trying to listen, listen, and listen some more until we've reached the bottom motive for the action. Here we have found the heart of the hurt that led to the bad decision.

2. *Invite your teen to reflect.* If sexual fantasy, shoplifting, or drinking does not satisfy the deep hunger within the heart of the young person, what will? It's a question worth pondering together. Whatever the issue, whatever the bottom-line need, people, things, and experiences will not fill the ache.

3. *Point your teen to Christ.* The parents of these young people can gently point out that no thing, no experience can ultimately fill the void they feel in their lives. Only hunger for God will—nothing more, nothing less. Parents will wisely share some of their own struggles with heart issues, and how God has been the only provider of satisfaction.

This level of communication is best bathed in both prayer and nurturance. Kids need comfort when they're hurting, and they need to be reassured of God's love, our love, and that we still believe in them.

A girl from Washington State wrote: "When everything seems its worst, just hug them and tell them how much you love them. Positive strokes . . . bring around the worst behavior. Love is always the answer." A twenty-four-year-old from Canada said that the one thing that made the difference for him was simply "their love and care."

Again it needs to be said that this deep level of reflection and communication won't be necessary in the aftermath of every bad news scenario that comes our way. When thirteen-year-old Johnny accidentally sends a baseball through a neighbor's window, it's not exactly a result of deep-seated inferiority or despair of life itself. We need to be sensitive to our kids, the situation, and their own level of pain in a given situation.

How God Handles Bad News

A twenty-year-old girl from Florida offers this advice to parents:

> Bring your child up with an understanding that he/she can choose to let God be *or* not be the Lord of his/her life in situations every day. Gradually, allow your child room to make more choices and decisions *and* mistakes as he/she gets older. But most of all, my advice is to always look at your parenting in comparison to how God parents you. Ask yourself questions like: Does God allow me room to make choices and mistakes? When I make a mistake, is God harsh with me?

There is considerable wisdom in her advice and in her questions. How does God handle bad news from *us*? He loves us, receives us, forgives us when we ask, and restores us. He does not blast us to pieces, as the trapper did his dog in the sad story that opened this chapter. God may allow the natural results of our bad decision to proceed, or He may, in His mercy, change the situation to exempt us from the otherwise natural consequences of our actions.

This brings us back to a biblical model of discipline. As we looked at Jesus' life in Chapter 2, we saw God incarnate actively loving, receiving, and caring for His followers, and treating their poor choices with compassion and mercy. There are many things we teach through our discipline. However, our reaction to bad news and the discipline that stems from it should flow from a relationship with God in which we not only experience the mercy and kindness of our loving Father for ourselves but freely pass that mercy and kindness on toward our young people as well.

It all sounds so good, and for many, by God's grace, it works. Yet sometimes, in some families, discipline just doesn't work. It seems as if we've done all the right things, had all the right attitudes, come at the whole enterprise in the attitude of Christ, and still we experience frustration and failure. Then what? To this vexing question we next turn our attention.

DISCUSSION QUESTIONS

1. How did your parents react to bad news?

2. Recall a recent situation in which you received bad news. What was the situation and what was your reaction?

3. The author states that a young person will react in one of five ways to bad news he/she brings or when it is discovered that you know the bad news from another source. Which reaction typifies your teenager: defensive, rationalizing, crying, bargaining, or a biblical response?

4. The author talks about the importance of comforting the hurting young person. How have you been able to comfort yours? Share an example.

5. Share one or two passages of Scripture in which you have found comfort in difficult times. (If you need a good one, try Isaiah 43:1b-3a.) How does this make you feel?

13

When Discipline Doesn't Work ———————— ✧

What do we do when discipline doesn't work? One Florida mother of three thought of a creative solution:

Dateline: Fort Lauderdale

GIRL PLAYS HOOKY SO MOM SUES THE SCHOOL

The mother of a truant 15-year-old has sued Deerfield Beach High School and five school officials, saying they have done nothing to help keep her daughter in school.

[The parent], 40, is asking for $2500 in damages from the school and from each of the officials. . . . She said she has gotten virtually no aid in forcing her daughter to go to school despite countless appeals for help.

"I'm tired of parents taking the blame," she said. "The school is not doing their job and they're breaking the law by not forcing her to go to school."

She said her two older daughters dropped out of Deerfield Beach High at 15 and 16. . . .[1]

Suing someone is a rather unusual way to cope with the disappointment of a rebellious teenager! However, most of us will not be so inclined to place the blame solely on the school, the church, the devil, or society in general.

Though perhaps not driven by such extreme circumstances as the mother from Florida, most of us parents will face times when we realize the discipline we are using just isn't working. For example:

• If we are authoritarian in our style of parenting, we might have one teenager who responds well while a sibling rebels. A democratic approach may have worked with both.

• Perhaps one of our three teenagers often expresses emotions as anger. If we don't recognize that a teenager who reacts with anger is different from one who doesn't, we're setting ourselves up for failure with that angry teenager. Here it is probably not the method of discipline that needs to be changed, but dealing with an underlying problem.

• If we have one teenager who has "special needs" (see below) and one who doesn't, we can't treat them alike. If we do, we'll have one kid who can handle normal freedom and take normal responsibilities. The other will give us fits by a seeming inability to handle what we consider normal and reasonable expectations.

• If we use negative and destructive kinds of discipline (e.g., yelling, threatening, etc.), some kids will endure this better than others. Put-downs may just roll off the back of your Type 2 son but upset your Type 1 daughter. If we use more positive discipline methods, both may respond well. Some kids seem relatively unaffected by our mistakes as parents, while others are destroyed by them.

We don't have to randomly guess at our problems, however. The first question we need to consider if discipline doesn't seem to be working is this: "Is my kid a *special-needs* teenager?"

Special Need, Special Challenge

Ultimate frustration is experienced by those who are trying their best to parent a "special needs" teenager—and they don't realize their son or daughter has a special need! With such a teenager, we can use all the right discipline methods, give all kinds of nurturance, even say all the "right" prayers, and still not achieve success. In this situation the special need must be addressed first—and this may mean several years of hard work parenting with the special need in mind.

If we are oblivious to a special-need situation, our attitude may eventually turn sour toward our difficult son or daughter. We may believe, and even say out loud, that they will amount to nothing good. Then our attitude becomes a self-fulfilling prophecy. What are some examples of these special needs?

Physical Handicap

In a sense this is the easiest of the special needs to deal with, because the need can be seen with our eyes. A teenager with an arm missing, or a deformed leg, or large birthmark on the face is different from his or her "normal looking" peers.

Most parents are quick to empathize with and be sensitive to the physical handicaps of their kids. No parent is going to expect his son to mow the lawn if he lost his leg in a car accident two months previously. But to expect nothing of a teen with a physical handicap can also be damaging to his or her sense of worth and self-esteem.

Since teenagers are so terribly aware of their bodies during these years, we can be certain they face quite an uphill struggle to have a decent self-image. If we are using discipline methods that place further burden on their already fragile self-esteem, we can easily push our physically handicapped young person into rebellion.

Mental Disorders

Here we enter a world where there seem to be more questions than answers. The human mind was designed by God as a wonderfully complex and awesome organ. However, the human brain and mind was not exempted from the fall of man described in Genesis 3. As sin and evil entered the world, the human mind became a potential residence for all manner of illness. Medical research is becoming aware of just how little it takes in terms of chemical imbalance or neurological malfunction to throw the mind off normal functioning.

Various kinds of phobias can arise as a young person matures. *Agoraphobia*, for example, is a fear of crowds. For this kind of young person, just going to school can become an almost overwhelmingly impossible task to face. We can discipline all we want, but it won't heal the mental disorder that results in the behavior that so mystifies us.

We know that, emotionally, teenagers tend to be high and low in quick succession. For a few, though, these highs and lows can become severe and prolonged. The parent of a *manic/depressive* young person will not solve the problem with a lecture or assigning Bible memorization. This malady is thought to be the result of a chemical imbalance within the brain.

A few teenagers will become *psychotic* and begin to lose touch with reality. If this isn't an example of bad things happening to good people, what is? Take a tour of the adolescent ward of your local mental hospital; you'll be amazed at how many mentally troubled kids are hidden away in hospitals like this. Some of them come from good Christian homes, as well.

The Jordans are gathered around their Christmas tree praying prayers of thanks for God's goodness to them. All five of their kids are grown now; four of them and Mr. and Mrs. Jordan are present today. They laugh, remember good times, and they will cry today too. They miss Chris, their fourth-born daughter. She was a wonderful Christian girl who wanted to be a missionary. When she was seventeen, however, they began to notice a change in her personality.

By high school graduation, the change had become obvious to those outside the family too. Chris was having trouble keeping a handle on the real world. She couldn't make real decisions or think realistically about life. She spoke of talking with angels, demons, and other spiritual entities.

This daughter and sister that they loved so much just started to come unglued mentally right before their eyes. Nothing "worked" on her—not discipline, not counseling, not prayer, not exorcism, not anything.

She has been institutionalized for over a year. This is her second Christmas away from home. Her Christian doctors offer the Jordans only slim hope of Chris ever being "normal" again.

If we, as parents, feel we are potentially facing a mental disorder in one of our teenagers, the proper step is to get qualified medical/professional help as soon as possible. Normal discipline methods don't necessarily work the same when we are facing a young person with this kind of need.

Less Obvious Special Needs

The following needs can create a great deal of frustration and pain for both teenagers and parents, but the reasons are not always obvious.

• *Learning disorders.* This will probably show up earlier than the teenage years. If not, however, the whole subject of school, grades, and fitting into the expectations of the school system will become a major source of frustration and conflict within the home. Discipline for poor grades won't help if the teenager is dyslexic and doesn't realize it.

• *Late bloomers.* Some teenage guys won't fully develop mentally into the "abstract reasoning" stage at all during their teenage years.[2] This will be a tremendous frustration to parents who will think to themselves again and again, "He's old enough to know better!" Those few who are not capable of changing their behavior "A" based on later consequence "B" will not respond well to disciplines that require that kind of reasoning.

• *PMS.* About 5–10 percent of women experience a premenstrual syndrome severe enough to have a substantial negative effect on their personal lives.[3] The onset of puberty is one of the four likely times in a woman's life when severe PMS will begin, if it develops at all. While only a few teenage girls will develop severe PMS, a larger number will be at least mildly affected by its symptoms. Severe PMS, with the symptoms evident from one to two weeks of the menstrual month, may show itself in extreme forgetfulness, clumsiness, or nearly uncontrollable rages at that time of the month. Disciplining a severely PMS-affected teenage girl will only generate hatred toward her parents. She doesn't need discipline, she needs understanding and possible treatment: a change of diet (caffeine, for example, substantially heightens PMS symptoms) or perhaps hormonal treatment.[4]

• *ADD teenagers.* Attention Deficit Disorder is the fancy name medicine has given what most people call being hyperactive. This will, of course, show up in the early years first, but if left untreated it can just about guarantee a difficult family situation for the parents and other siblings. These kinds of kids need a great amount of structure and guidance to make it through the expectations of their increased age. Parent counseling, behavior modification, special education, and, as a last resort, medication are all tools that are used when it becomes apparent that a young person has ADD.[5]

• *Childhood trauma.* Different kids carry different scars from their past. A teenager whose mother was an alcoholic while pregnant will probably be born with FAS—fetal alcohol syndrome. This implies major behavioral and learning problems a decade or two down the line. Divorce, a death in the family, sexual abuse—all are capable of bumping the teenager into the "special needs" category. What works with "normal" kids may not work at all with these scared and scarred young people.

If we think our teenager might have a special need, the important thing is to *get help*. We can go to our pastor for suggestions about Christian counseling; we can go to our doctor for medical or psychological evaluation. There is help out there! As we prayerfully and faithfully use the resources God has given us to find that help, we show our love for our young person and our care that he or she turns out all right.

After pondering all this, if we feel our teenager is *not* a special-needs kid, we may breathe a sigh of relief—but still feel frustration over discipline that doesn't seem to work. How are we to think then?

When Discipline Doesn't Work With "Normal" Teenagers

Some home appliances come with a troubleshooting guide in the back of the owner's manual. Got a problem you can't figure out? Go to the manual. At your wits' end because discipline methods, even good ones, aren't working with your teenager? Help! Where's the owner's manual! We can't exactly take a kid back to the manufacturer for a refund or a discount on the next model. However, here's a troubleshooting guide to help you think through your problem:

Thinking Wrongly That We're Doing It Right
Say what? Sometimes we may think we are using a discipline method the right way when we really aren't at all. This is a common mistake parents of young children make.

"Joey, if you can't stop whining, you must go to your room."

Little Joey, age three and a half, starts crying and sits down on the floor.

"I said, go to your room!"

Joey shakes his head and begins to scream. When his mom starts to pick him up, he wiggles free and runs into the family room.

Joey's mom lets him go, thinking that she has stopped his whining. But Joey was showing her he was still in control by going into the family room instead of his room. She entered into a power struggle and lost.

The same mother, a decade later, may make a similar mistake.

> "Joey, if you don't clean your room before supper you won't eat."
>
> Joey didn't clean his room and didn't eat supper that night. Much to her surprise, he still didn't clean his room. So, she proclaimed the discipline method a failure and resumed normal meal service the next day. She was convinced it was the method that failed, not herself.

Sometimes we need to think through a situation more thoroughly. Talk it through with your spouse or close friend. They might be insightful enough to point out our mistakes.

The mother in the above example made two mistakes. As we have already mentioned, she thought she was doing things right, when she wasn't. Her second mistake was that she didn't follow through on consequences.

Good at Everything Except Follow-Through

If you don't follow through on consequences, your "discipline" will have no effect because your kids know you'll either forget about it or back down. Some kids will only change their behavior if they see that their parents mean business. Kids who might be motivated by the prospect of long-term consequences (like lost privileges or more chores), will not bother to change their behavior if there is no follow-through.

This does not overlook the possibility that we may change our mind about the discipline based on further reflection or new information. We may also decide to grant mercy for the sake of mercy. If either of these is the case, we need to communicate clearly to our son or daughter that the discipline is being removed and why.

Failure to clearly communicate can result in our teenager believing that we are simply weak-willed and that we will probably back down next time, too, if they hold out long enough. Lack of communication sets us up for future failure.

Related to poor follow-through is the fact that some discipline methods are clearly better suited to certain kinds of parents and not others. The Parental Strike, for example, requires a parent who has a strong will and sense of dedication to a task. The Family Council requires at least one parent who is outgoing enough to lead a meeting successfully. If we pick discipline methods we are ill-equipped to carry out, we either have to improve the skill necessary to do it or find a different discipline method. We need to choose one that is still positive but that we can actually accomplish.

Nonmotivating Motivators
Different young people aren't motivated by the same things. Shy teenagers aren't motivated by social restriction because they make few outside plans anyway. Eleven-year-old boys who can't think about a thought won't be motivated by being told, "If you do poorly in school you might not get into college!"

All teenagers have their own sets of likes and dislikes. They have their own opinions about what is important to them. Be sure to think of your young person as an individual when you choose something to motivate him or her. Just because something worked on one of your other kids doesn't mean it will motivate the next one.

Crippling Self-Image
A poor self-image may show itself in any number of ways. Bill may lie to his friends at school about how much money he has or about what he did during the summer; Cherie might get drunk on the weekends. Bill wants his friends to think he is important and Cherie wants to fit in with other kids and not be weird. Parents who discipline the lying or the drunkenness may miss the underlying reason for the behavior. The behavior won't change unless the root cause changes. The best approach is to discipline gently while you set in motion a plan to improve your teen's self-image.

Different Personality Traits

Sometimes we can trace a teenager's misbehavior to his or
her personality. For example:

Two sisters who live in the same bedroom are likely to
have conflicts if one is organized (typical of Type 1) and one
is messy (typical of Type 2). Discipline won't stop their
fighting; the setup is designed to be a failure. In this situation
parents would need to divide the room clearly so each has
her own private space, as well as work with the kids indi-
vidually. Perhaps the messy one could be motivated through
a positive discipline method to improve how she keeps her
part of the room.

Again, the best solution in this situation is to take a gentle
approach in our discipline and work at smoothing out
underlying causes of the problem.

Misread Anger

When faced with a problem, some young people—particularly Type 2 teenagers—respond in anger. Their anger is
a mask for their true emotions, whether they are fear, disappointment, or hurt feelings.

Joey, now age fifteen, faced his mother who was finishing
her stern lecture on how wrong he was to not come home by
nine o'clock on a school night.

"It wasn't my fault!" he yelled. "I was trying to help Pete
fix his car, and we had to finish what we were working on.
Just leave me alone." (*Slam* went his bedroom door.) What
he didn't tell his mom was that they were also playing with
some gasoline in the garage. It caught fire and nearly turned
into a disaster.

Joey knows his mother goes crazy when he does something wrong. He hates her lectures—despises them, actually. He has learned that the best defense with her is a good
offense. He was truly fearful of what she would do if she
knew the truth, so he left out the real reason, defended
himself with his own rage, and cut off his mom by leaving
the room.

The teenager who yells and says, "It wasn't my fault!" may be expressing fear. He needs to be gently taught that he doesn't have to show his fear that way. If we yell back and load on the discipline, we teach him that he had good reason to be defensive. And we set in motion a pattern for future miscommunication.

The next time Joey has problems he's going to look back on this event and think, "Am I ever in trouble. Mom was awfully mad the last time I was late—and she didn't even know about the fire. It worked pretty well to get madder than she was and then cut out—guess I'll try that again."

Soon Joey's mom begins to label him as defensive and rebellious. Then there is even less motivation for him to change. His mom won't see any good that he does when she is so busy focusing on the bad. And so the pattern continues.

Joey acted defensively, but underneath he was really fearful about what his mom would do or say. If she had realized this she could have said, "Joey, I understand that things don't always go right when you're trying to work on Pete's car. But we have an agreement about when you're supposed to be home on a school night. What do you think should have happened in this case?"

This response leaves an open door for discussion. Together they can think about what he should have done when he realized he would be late.

We parents need to respond gently and uncritically, remembering, "Love is patient, love is kind . . . is not easily angered, it keeps no record of wrongs" (1 Corinthians 13:4, 5). Over time, our teenagers will be able to come to us and tell us calmly, "I made a mistake, this is what I did . . . and I know it was my fault." They will be able to do this because they will have learned that we will not respond in anger, so they don't need to defend themselves.

Some teenagers may use anger to express disappointment, sadness, or hurt feelings. Their anger triggers our anger and we try to discipline their anger, making matters worse. With God's help, we should stop reacting in anger ourselves, and instead try to draw out their true feelings. We can help them see that if they are sad, we can comfort them, or at least not judge them. If they are angry, they cut off the comfort and sympathy they could have received.

In the above example Joey's mom might have also identified his anger and upset as being an overreaction to the frustration of car parts that don't fit right. Was something else going on? An alert parent might have said, "Joey, you seem very upset. Did something happen over at Pete's tonight? Do you want to talk about it?"

When we calmly ask questions that will help a teenager identify his or her true emotions, we open the door to good communication and bring hope to both ourselves and our teenager.

Discipline will never stop anyone's defensive or angry responses. Perhaps there will need to be discipline, but it needs to be gentle and the situation must always be dealt with in the context of the teen's true emotions.

This form of gentle discipline and guidance will have lifelong results in the young person. As an adult, he or she will be able to go to a boss or a spouse or a child and say, "I made a mistake . . ." or, "I'm feeling disappointed about what happened."

Mismatched Parenting Style

The statistics couldn't be much clearer: the older the teenager, the less successful the autocratic/authoritarian style of parenting will be. When combined with a lot of love, it can work pretty well with a twelve-year-old, but not with a kid who's eighteen. If your discipline isn't working, review your parenting style and make sure it's what it needs to be.

Who Are the Candidates for Rebellion?

In reviewing the above reasons discipline may not work with a "normal" teenager, we should also be aware of the type of teenager who will be most affected by them: the strong-willed teenager! Type 2 kids are often the ones who are this way.

Three of the mistakes listed above could result in open rebellion by your own strong-willed son or daughter.

1. Wrong Parenting Style

A strong-willed teenager isn't afraid to challenge or step over the line. He's probably had lots of practice as a child. The authoritative style will not go over well with him. This young person needs freedom and room to develop; he needs us to let go. If we don't give it willingly, the strong-willed young person will not be afraid to just take it.

2. Crippling Self-Image

A meek teenager may be afraid to turn to drugs or alcohol to boost his self-image; a parent pleaser might worry about disappointing parents. A strong-willed teenager with a crippled self-image, however, is probably accustomed to disappointing her parents. In fact, people have come to expect her to do just that, so rebellion is a likely option. In a perverse kind of way, it may even boost self-esteem.

3. Misread Anger

The teenagers who are most likely to react defensively are the strong-willed ones. As we have seen already, our angry reaction builds their defensiveness and their hostility toward us. After a while, open rebellion becomes an easy step.

Understanding these insights will help us get a handle on where the problem really is and how to attack it. It may take a long time before we see improvement, however. In the meantime, we must simply hang in there.

There are going to be times when we feel as if we have failed with our teenagers. Most families with teenagers face a crisis of one sort or another. What resources do we have, as Christian parents, when things are not turning out very well?

Hanging in There

In the early days of parenting, we might think that severe problems with a teenager just couldn't happen in our home. Expected or not, a wayward, rebellious young person can turn a formerly happy family into a miniature hell. We cry out to God and ask why; we don't understand the reasons. We don't see any purpose in the crisis. We see no way God's name is being honored or His Kingdom advanced. We experience a universe from which all traces of God seem to have vanished.

We feel like Job in the Old Testament. But his questions weren't answered by God, and God is under no obligation to answer our questions. There may be times when we feel empty and alone. Yet, in time, our minds may begin to accept this suffering as one way God teaches us.

This is not to say that God causes our teenagers to go astray. He does not cause bad situations, but He can use them for His glory and our instruction. Our teenagers have free will; despite good parenting and even the work of the Holy Spirit in their lives, young people choose of their own free will to accept or reject God and the values of their parents.

We may have a lot of guilt as parents. Looking back on the mistakes we've made, we may see we're reaping what we have sown. A crisis may make us realize we have actually sinned as parents. Our put-downs, threats, and yelling are a far cry from the ideal of the family as a Christian support group we see in the New Testament.

If this is the case, we need to admit our failure to the Lord and obtain His forgiveness. The promise in 1 John 1:9—that God will forgive and cleanse us when we confess our sin—applies to parents too! If we have sinned against our teenagers, we need to admit our failure to them as well.

Any commuter in a big city knows the frustration of sitting on a freeway that has become a parking lot. It's no fun and can seem like forever before one makes any forward progress. Parenting a teenager can also feel like sitting in a traffic jam. We know where we want to go, but our progress is blocked. We may eventually turn on the radio to get the traffic report and even see the traffic copter pass overhead. We realize that the people up there have a far different perspective—they can see where the problem is, how far traffic is backed up, and about how long it's going to take before people on the ground are moving normally again.

This is a picture of the difference we have as Christian parents. We can look up and understand our heavenly Father sees the whole picture. He knows where we're going; He knows what's blocking the kind of family He wants us to have. He knows how long it's going to take before we're making progress again.

In a traffic jam, the problem, well beyond our view, often begins to clear out long before we notice any difference. It can be the same way spiritually and in problems with our teenagers. We may feel completely stymied and stalled, yet up ahead, well beyond our view, our loving Father is guiding and leading. He is working in our lives and the lives of our teenagers.

We may feel like David when he wrote in Psalm 116:3, 4:

The cords of death entangled me, the anguish of the grave came upon me; I was overcome by trouble and sorrow. Then I called on the name of the LORD: "O LORD, save me!"

In answer to our cry for help, the Lord may sometimes change the circumstances and "things work out." Other times, however, He changes *us* and uses the pain and stress to produce in us a peace that only comes from the Holy Spirit in our lives—a peace that can enable us to say, even before we see any solution:

The LORD is gracious and righteous; our God is full of compassion. . . . Be at rest once more, O my soul, for the LORD has been good to you.

Psalm 116:5, 7

DISCUSSION QUESTIONS

1. Do you have a "special needs" teenager? What do you feel is the special need?

2. If discipline isn't working well for you, and your teenager does not have a special need, which of the reasons listed might apply to your situation?

3. If your son or daughter often reacts in anger, what emotions do you think this anger may be masking? How can you help bring true emotions out, instead of the anger?

4. What are some examples in your life of bad things that God has used for good?

5. Open your Bible to James 3:13–18. Compare a lifestyle with godly wisdom to one without. As you think about your family, in what area or about what issue do you need His wisdom now?

Appendix

Original research provided the basis of much of the material to be found in Chapters 5–8. College-age young people who were Christians were asked to complete a two-page survey and answer questions as they reflected on the discipline they received between the ages of eleven and nineteen. The survey was completed by 385 people from nineteen cities in ten states and one province of Canada. All regions of the country were represented in the survey.

The following provides the content of the actual survey instrument used.

QUESTIONNAIRE

I. About You . . .

1. Your current age is ___ Sex: ❏ Male ❏ Female

2. Check the characteristics, both positive and negative, that are generally descriptive of you in the last two or three years.

- avoids conflict
- blames others
- charming
- conscientious
- critical
- engaging
- good salesperson
- independent

- list maker
- manipulative
- many friends
- mediator
- more socially mature than peers
- people person
- perfectionistic

- rebel
- reliable
- scholarly
- serious
- show-off
- very loyal to peer group
- well organized

II. About Your Parents . . .

Researchers have identified different "styles of parenting." Take a moment to familiarize yourself with these terms:

Style A: Autocratic/Authoritarian
Parents do not allow teenager to express opinions or make decisions about their lives, *or* while son/daughter may contribute opinion, parents always make final decision.

Style B: Democratic/Equalitarian
Teens contribute freely on issues relevant to their behavior, but final decisions often subject to parent approval, *or* parents and teens essentially equal in decision-making authority.

Style C: Permissive/Ignoring
Teen assumes a more active and influential role in decision making and considers, but not always abides by, parental preferences, *or* parent shows little or no interest in directing teenagers' behavior.

4. Which style (A, B, or C) typified your parents during the following three periods of your life:

Ages 11–13 ___
Ages 14–16 ___
Ages 17–19 ___

III. About Your Parents Disciplining You . . .

5. When or if your parents were generally successful in their discipline, punishment, or correction of you (that is, if you obeyed and accepted their discipline), to what do you attribute this success? (Use other side if you need to.)

6. When or if your parents were generally unsuccessful in their discipline, punishment, or correction of you (that is, you did not obey and accept their discipline), to what do you attribute this lack of success? (Use other side if you need to.)

7. It is certainly possible that there were periods in your life when your parents were more successful in their discipline/punishment/correction of you than at others. Place a check in the appropriate boxes below:

	Ages 11–13	Ages 14–16	Ages 17–19
Generally successful			
Generally unsuccessful			

8. Several methods of discipline/punishment/correction are listed below. In each of the three age categories, put a "+" for the methods your parents used that were successful, put a "-" for those that were unsuccessful, and put a "0" for those that were not used.

	Ages 11–13	Ages 14–16	Ages 17–19
Spanking/Hitting			
Lecturing			
Yelling			
Threatening			
Positive Rewards			
Loss of Privileges			
Restriction			
More Chores/Work			
Bible Study/Memorization			
Community Service			
Cut in Allowance			

	Ages 11–13	Ages 14–16	Ages 17–19
Bribery			
Put-downs/Humiliation			
Ignoring/Silent Treatment			
Parental Strike			
Contracting			
Family Council			
Forced Apologies			

9. In your family you were:
    ___ first-born
    ___ second-born
    ___ third-born
    ___ other _____

10. If you have any advice you'd like to give parents about disciplining their teenagers, please do so on the back of this sheet.

The responses to the above survey were entered and tabulated using the industry standard for behavioral research, the Statistical Package for the Social Sciences (SPSS).

Relevant results that are not already included in the text are listed here.

Survey Question 1

Age: 21 and under: 58.7 percent
22 and over: 41.3 percent
Sex: males: 50.0 percent
females: 50.0 percent

Survey Question 2

Type 1, 2, and 3 characteristics were noted on the survey. If respondents checked more Type 1 characteristics than either Type 2 or Type 3, they were designated "Type 1." The various types were as follows:

Type 1: 41.8 percent
Type 2: 41.0 percent
Type 3: 8.3 percent

Survey Question 4

PARENTING STYLES AND THEIR FREQUENCY OF USE (BY PERCENT)			
Age	Autocratic/ Authoritarian	Democratic/ Equalitarian	Permissive/ Ignoring
Eleven to Thirteen	57.7	38.3	3.9
Fourteen to Sixteen	25.6	64.8	9.7
Seventeen to Nineteen	10.2	52.5	37.3

Survey Question 7

Percentage of kids who evaluated their parents' discipline as being "generally successful" when used on them.

Ages Eleven to Thirteen   87.3 percent
Ages Fourteen to Sixteen   69.1 percent
Ages Seventeen to Nineteen   67.0 percent

Survey Question 7 combined with Survey Question 4

PARENTING STYLES AND DEGREE OF SUCCESS AT DIFFERENT AGES (BY PERCENT)			
Style	Ages 11–13	Ages 14–16	Ages 17–19
Autocratic/Authoritarian	87.3	58.4	37.5
Democratic/Equalitarian	90.1	80.3	79.7
Permissive/Ignoring	57.1	41.7	63.6

Survey Question 8 combined with Questions 1 and 2

**DISCIPLINE METHOD THAT "WORKED"
WHEN USED WITH AGES 11–13 (BY PERCENT)**

Method	Type 1	Type 2	Type 3	Guys	Girls
1. Bible Study/ Memorization	73	75	—*	67	80
2. Bribery	50	45	—	—	—**
3. Community Service	61	53	—	50	70
4. Contracting	58	74	—	57	81
5. Cut in Allowance	64	90	—	78	86
6. Family Council	86	78	—	80	88
7. Forced Apology	40	39	—	46	43
8. Ignoring/Silent	30	30	—	33	35
9. Lecture	81	70	88	75	83
10. Loss of Privileges	91	93	95	87	98
11. More Chores	77	80	—	78	82
12. Parental Strike	27	41	—	44	50
13. Positive Rewards	89	95	95	94	93
14. Put-downs/ Humiliation	29	23	—	27	32
15. Restriction	86	86	95	84	91
16. Spanking	88	81	95	91	83
17. Threatening	53	53	—	58	53
18. Yelling	37	50	—	52	45

*Since only 8 percent (thirty-two cases) of the total sample indicated they were Type 3, most discipline methods were reported to be used in an insufficient number of homes to be statistically significant. The percentage is given if the discipline method was used in at least twenty cases.

**Inadvertently omitted in the computer analysis.

DISCIPLINE METHOD THAT "WORKED" WHEN USED WITH AGES 14–16 (BY PERCENT)

Method	Type 1	Type 2	Type 3	Guys	Girls
1. Bible Study/ Memorization	65	78	—	—*	—
2. Bribery	—	38	—	—	—
3. Community Service	—	—	—	—	—
4. Contracting	—	—	—	—	—
5. Cut in Allowance	—	70	—	52	80
6. Family Council	83	80	—	77	84
7. Forced Apology	33	36	—	42	27
8. Ignoring/Silent	27	28	—	—	46
9. Lecture	76	69	75	77	79
10. Loss of Privileges	79	87	90	85	92
11. More Chores	62	82	—	72	77
12. Parental Strike	—	—	—	—	—
13. Positive Rewards	93	90	100	95	96
14. Put-downs/ Humiliation	18	17	—	8	25
15. Restriction	66	85	—	87	86
16. Spanking	43	46	—	62	60
17. Threatening	43	38	—	36	56
18. Yelling	30	30	—	32	42

*Blanks mean the method was used in an insufficient number of homes with this type or sex to be statistically significant.

DISCIPLINE METHOD THAT "WORKED" WHEN USED WITH AGES 17–19 (BY PERCENT)

Method	Type 1	Type 2	Type 3	Guys	Girls
1. Bible Study/ Memorization	—*	65	—	—	—
2. Bribery	—	—	—	—	—
3. Community Service	—	—	—	—	—
4. Contracting	73	75	—	71	82
5. Cut in Allowance	—	66	—	—	—
6. Family Council	50	52	—	48	55
7. Forced Apology	—	—	—	—	—
8. Ignoring/Silent	—	50	—	—	—
9. Lecture	63	70	86	79	79
10. Loss of Privileges	74	75	—	84	87
11. More Chores	53	75	—	73	76
12. Parental Strike	—	—	—	—	—
13. Positive Rewards	90	89	—	96	89
14. Put-downs/ Humiliation	33	40	—	—	32
15. Restriction	45	69	—	70	75
16. Spanking	12	22	—	—	38
17. Threatening	29	23	—	40	30
18. Yelling	13	22	—	26	23

*Blanks mean the method was used in an insufficient number of homes with this type or sex to be statistically significant.

Survey Question 8 combined with Questions 1 and 2

DISCIPLINE METHOD AND PERCENT OF FAMILIES WHERE USED ACCORDING TO "STYLE," AGES 11–13		
Method	Autocratic/ Authoritarian	Democratic/* Equalitarian
1. Bible Study/Memorization	16	13
2. Bribery	11	11
3. Community Service	8	8
4. Contracting	11	7
5. Cut in Allowance	18	24
6. Family Council	27	31
7. Forced Apology	35	24
8. Ignoring/Silent	22	17
9. Lecture	77	80
10. Loss of Privileges	67	62
11. More Chores	42	42
12. Parental Strike	12	9
13. Positive Rewards	59	70
14. Put-downs/Humiliation	27	21
15. Restriction	62	51
16. Spanking	71	58
17. Threatening	49	34
18. Yelling	69	58

*The permissive/ignoring approach is omitted from this table because it was used in so few families with this age young person.

Survey Question 9

First-born	41.1 percent
Second-born	26.6 percent
Third-born	14.3 percent
Other	18.0 percent

NOTES

Chapter 1. It Really Matters

1. Ann C. Roark, "Latchkey Children in Jeopardy," in *The Seattle Times*, September 6, 1989.

2. Fitzhugh Dodson, *How to Discipline with Love* (New York: Rawson, Wade Publishers, Inc., 1977), p. 1.

3. "The Gentle Art of Discipline," in *Parents*, April 1986, no author listed, p. 80.

Chapter 2. The Bible and Discipline

1. Probably the most complete description of this approach to the Christian life is found in *The Normal Christian Life* by Watchman Nee (London: Victory Press, 1957).

Chapter 3. Parenting Styles

1. Definitions of parenting styles adapted from Kathleen S. Berger, *The Developing Person Through Childhood and Adolescence* (New York: Worth Publishers Inc., 1986), p. 531.

2. Dorothy Rogers, *Adolescents and Youth*, Fifth Edition (Englewood Cliffs, New Jersey: Prentice Hall, 1985), pp. 239, 240.

3. Peter L. Benson and Dorothy L. Williams, *The Quicksilver Years* (San Francisco: Harper and Row, 1987), pp. 189, 196.

4. Ibid., p. 195.

5. Rogers, *Adolescents*, p. 244.

6. Benson, *Quicksilver Years*, p. 187.

7. Ibid., p. 195.

Chapter 4. EIGHTEEN DIFFERENT DISCIPLINE METHODS

1. Fitzhugh Dodson, *How to Discipline with Love* (New York: Rawson, Wade Publishers, Inc., 1977), pp. 22–29.

2. For a book-length treatment of the subject of negotiating with your kids with positive results for all concerned, see: Bradley Bucher, *Winning Them Over* (New York: Times Books, 1987).

3. For a full explanation of the Family Council, see: James Oraker, *Almost Grown* (New York: Harper and Row, 1980), pp. 120–126.

4. Kenneth Blanchard and Spencer Johnson, *The One Minute Manager* (New York: William Morrow and Co., 1982).

5. Bruno Bettelheim, "Punishment Versus Discipline," in *The Atlantic*, November 1985, p. 52.

Chapter 5. AGES ELEVEN TO THIRTEEN, PART I

1. List of characteristics derived and adapted from Kevin Leman, *The Birth Order Book* (Old Tappan, New Jersey: Fleming H. Revell, 1985).

2. Ibid.

3. James R. Oraker, *Almost Grown* (New York: Harper and Row, 1980), p. 87.

4. David Elkind, "Understanding the Young Adolescent," in *Adolescence*, 1978, 13(40), pp. 127–134.

5. John P. Hill and Grayson N. Holmbeck, "Disagreements About Rules in Families with Seventh-Grade Girls and Boys," in *Journal of Youth and Adolescence*, Vol. 16, No. 3, 1987, p. 221.

6. Ibid., pp. 230, 231.

7. Peter L. Benson and Dorothy L. Williams, *The Quicksilver Years* (San Francisco: Harper and Row, 1987), p. 186.

Chapter 6. Ages Eleven to Thirteen, Part II

1. A helpful and full treatment of the Parental Strike may be found in Robert and Jean Bayard's book, *How to Deal with Your Acting-Up Teenager* (New York: Evans Co., 1983), pp. 163–174.

Chapter 7. Ages Fourteen to Sixteen

1. Anthony Campolo, *Growing Up in America* (Grand Rapids: Zondervan, 1989), p. 36.

2. James Oraker, *Almost Grown* (New York: Harper and Row, 1980), p. 91.

3. Jane Norman and Myron Harris, *The Private Life of the American Teenager* (New York: Rawson, Wade Publishers, Inc., 1987), p. 227.

4. Ibid., p. 232.

5. Ibid., p. 233.

6. David Preusser, Allan Williams, and Adrian Lund, "Parental Role in Teenage Driving," in *Journal of Youth and Adolescence*, Vol. 14, No. 2, 1985, p. 81.

7. Norman, *Private Life*, p. 241.

Chapter 8. Ages Seventeen to Nineteen

1. Gary Luft and Gwendolyn Sorell, "Parenting Style and Parent-Adolescent Religious Value Consensus" in *Journal of Adolescence*, Vol. 2, No. 1, p. 53.

2. Ibid.

3. Thomas Gordon, *Parent Effectiveness Training* (New York: New American Library, 1975).

4. Tommie J. Hamner and Pauline H. Turner, *Parenting in Contemporary Society* (Englewood Cliffs, New Jersey: Prentice Hall, 1985), p. 87.

Chapter 9. An Ounce of Prevention

1. Adapted from Larry Richards, *Youth Ministry in the Local Church* (Grand Rapids: Zondervan, 1972), pp. 139–142.

2. Jay Kesler, ed., *Parents and Teenagers* (Wheaton: Victor Books, 1984), p. 445.

Chapter 11. REGAINING CONTROL

1. Adapted from Robert and Jean Bayard, *How to Deal with Your Acting-Up Teenager* (New York: Evans Co., 1983), pp. 138–140.
2. Nathan H. Azrin and Richard M. Fox, *Toilet Training in Less Than a Day* (New York: Simon & Schuster, 1974).

Chapter 12. HANDLING BAD NEWS

1. As told by Dan Webster, National Youth Workers Convention, Chicago, Illinois, October 17, 1985.
2. David Swartz, *Dancing with Broken Bones* (Colorado Springs: NavPress, 1987).
3. Adapted from Jay Kesler, ed., *Parents and Teenagers* (Wheaton: Victor Books, 1984), p. 571.
4. Kevin Huggins, *Parenting Adolescents* (Colorado Springs: NavPress, 1989), pp. 229–231.

Chapter 13. WHEN DISCIPLINE DOESN'T WORK

1. Deborah P. Work of the *Fort Lauderdale News & Sun Sentinel*, as carried in *The Seattle Times*, November 23, 1989, p. C7.
2. Kathleen S. Berger, *The Developing Person Through Childhood and Adolescence* (New York: Worth Publishers, 1986), p. 495.
3. Ronald V. Norris, *Premenstrual Syndrome* (New York: Berkley Books, 1983), p. 3.
4. Ibid., p. 204.
5. John Rosemond, "Parenting: Is Your Child Hyperactive?" in *Better Homes and Gardens*, April 1989, p. 38.